Angelica

Camomile

Marjoram

Sage

Sesame

Dill

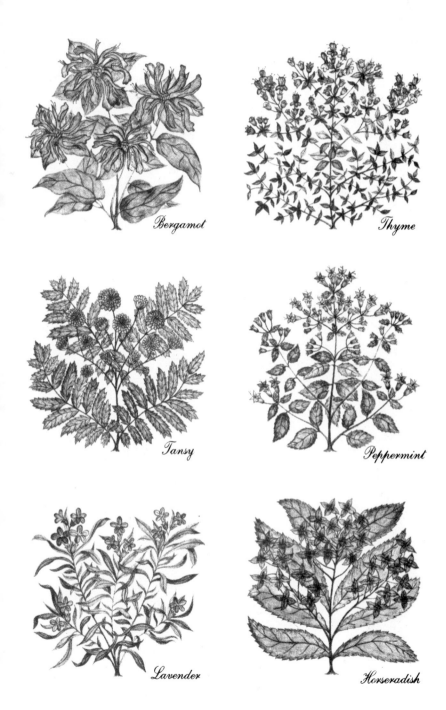

Bergamot

Thyme

Tansy

Peppermint

Lavender

Horseradish

Growing and Using Herbs and Spices

Growing and Using Herbs and Spices

MILO MILORADOVICH

Dover Publications, Inc.
New York

Published in Canada by General Publishing Company, Ltd., 30
Lesmill Road, Don Mills, Toronto, Ontario.
Published in the United Kingdom by Constable and Company,
Ltd., 10 Orange Street, London WC2H 7EG.

This Dover edition, first published in 1986, is a slightly abridged
republication of the work first published in 1952 by Doubleday &
Company, Inc. under the title *The Home Garden Book of Herbs &
Spices*. The list of suppliers of herb plants and seeds which appeared
in the 1952 edition has been deleted here.

Manufactured in the United States of America
Dover Publications, Inc., 31 East 2nd Street, Mineola, N.Y. 11501

Library of Congress Cataloging in Publicaton Data

Miloradovich, Milo.
  Growing and using herbs and spices.

  Reprint. Originally published: The home garden book of herbs
and spices. Garden City, N.Y. : Doubleday, 1952.
  Includes index.
  1. Herbs.   2. Herb gardening.   3. Spices.   4. Nature craft.
I. Title.
SB351.H5M54   1986   635'.7   85-27589
ISBN 0-486-25058-X (pbk.)

To Louise

. . . . . who so loves a garden

Herbs, too, she knew, and well of each could speak,
That in her garden sipped the silvery dew;

   . . .

The tufted Basil, pun-provoking Thyme,
Fresh Baum, and Marygold of cheerful hue,

   . . .

And Marjoram Sweet, in shepherd's posie found,
And Lavender, whose spikes of azure bloom
Shall be, erewhile, in arid bundles bound,
To lurk amidst the labours of her loom,
And crown her kerchief clean with mickle rare perfume.

William Shenstone
1714–63

Many Thanks

are expressed here to all those who have given me permission to make use of original designs, sketches, planting plans, and research material for inclusion in this book. My thanks especially to *Mr. J. A. Martin,* Associate Horticulturist of Clemson Agricultural College; to *Mrs. Philip W. Foster* of Falls Village, Connecticut; to *Mrs. Frances R. Williams* of Winchester, Massachusetts; also to *Mrs. Percy Cashmore* of Westport, Connecticut, for suggesting that I include the unique records of Mrs. Williams' research; and to *Mrs. Oliver B. Capen* of Bedford, New York, for her helpful co-operation with the member-units of The Herb Society of America.

Appreciation is given to *Mrs. Mortimer J. Fox* of Mount Kisco, New York, and to *Helen M. Whitman* of Salem Center, New York, for permission to reproduce any and all parts of their original design and planting plans of The Herb Society of America—The New York Unit's Herb Garden—which is in The New York Botanical Garden, Bronx, New York.

Also many thanks to the following Clevelanders: to *Mrs. Kenneth W. Gage,* of the Western Reserve Herb Society, which is a unit of The Herb Society of America, and to *Mr. Arnold M. Davis,* Director of The Garden Center of Greater Cleveland, for their co-operation in making it possible to include the line drawings and plans of the Wade Park Herb Garden. The original garden plan was adapted by *Henry Prée,* Landscape Architect, and honorary member of the Western Reserve Herb Society, from an old English garden plan shown in "The Compleat Gardener, 1704." The original planting plans were prepared by *Mrs. Alexander C. Brown* and *Mrs. Donald Gray.*

The line drawings in this book of the Wade Park Herb Garden were selected and prepared from recent plans drawn by *Mrs. Seth R. Cummings.* All those mentioned in connection with the Wade Park Herb Garden are members of the Western Reserve Herb Society, a Unit of The Herb Society of America.

Warm appreciation is given also to *Margaret S. Biggerstaff,* Director of Promotion for The New York Botanical Garden. Her genuine enthusiasm was of invaluable assistance in cooperation with that of *Mr. Justine V. McCarthy* in securing the original herb and spice-blossom sketches of *Aldo Becci* of the Delano Studios, Setauket, Long Island.

Thanks are especially expressed for the sketches: twelve, of the series of twenty-four which appear on the end papers, have been especially drawn for this volume.

Milo Miloradovich

Introductory Comment

As promised in my previous book on culinary herbs and spices, this garden book has been planned as a companion volume. The historical backgrounds and legendry of the same culinary herbs and spices are given with their many fragrant household uses. I have included the descriptive paragraphs on all the spices even though the majority of the vines, trees (blossoms and fruits), or plants from which the spices are prepared, are grown on large plantations in the tropics. If a spice-plant, however, is adaptable to growing in a garden in the warmer climates, then the detailed gardening instructions are also given.

The tropical and semi-tropical trees, vines, and plants are included, not only because of their unusual beauty, but also that all homemakers, gourmets, gardeners, and all readers might have as compact and complete a source of reference on the culinary herbs and spices as possible without having to search in numerous places for answers to the many questions surrounding this fascinating subject. To the best of my knowledge, these companion volumes are the only modern books which include the gardening details, the legendry, and the culinary histories of both subjects: herbs *and* spices.

The dominant colors and shades of both the foliage and the blossoms of the plants are grouped together for quick and easy reference in special lists so those who may wish to plan herb gardens according to specific color schemes may do so. Other lists have been prepared for the selection of herbs which thrive in various sections in the garden and under various

11

conditions. The listed nurseries and herb gardens from which seed and seedlings may be purchased have been divided into groups of geographical locations. This insures receiving the seedlings while still fresh and also gives the purchaser plants which have been conditioned to similar temperatures within a given locality. Though shipping healthy seedlings a long distance does not always necessarily injure them, it is best to be able to transplant them as soon as possible after they have been taken from the original seed-bed or garden.

Everything connected with herbs and spices can be a continual source of delight: growing one's own herbs in a small garden, in a window box, or even in a single pot on a window sill; reading of the herbs' and spices' romantic and often dramatic histories; and being intrigued by the mysticism, the superstitions, and the fantastic legends surrounding so many of them.

A small and simple herb garden can be a place of rare attractiveness and fragrant beauty. It need include but a few of the favorite and more popular, easily grown herbs. Often designed with but the thought of having hours of quiet pleasure and the uncomplicated joy of digging in the earth, the beginning of many such a garden has developed into a successful enterprise for more than one herb enthusiast.

The majority of both amateur and professional gardeners agree that scarcely anything can compare with the joy of watching the hardy perennials make their reappearances year after year. I have seen them push their tiny green leaves through a light snowfall, long before the calendar indicated that springtime was near. I have picked the crisp, deep-green sprigs of curly-parsley when its leaves, shimmering with a thin coating of ice, have glistened in the northwestern sunshine of a brisk winter morning.

A simple beginning and a small one, planting but 6 or 8 of the herbs most easily grown, will, in practically every instance, prove the most satisfactory and inspiring. Actual success with a few favorites can do more to lead one into the exciting adventure of experimenting with and in growing more varieties of herbs, than can many hours of just reading about them.

Actually working in a garden, or merely growing herbs in a window box, acquaints one with their idiosyncrasies as well as with their particular characteristics and fragrances. The shades and textures of the leaves, the colors of the flowering tips, the qualities of the seed and the berries become as familiar as a close intimate friend.

Your own personal selection of the first herbs will give you a more pleasurable satisfaction than you can possibly anticipate. Herbs react most sensitively to the gardener and to the various soils, climates, and degrees of sunshine. Discover all about herbs for yourself and there is no telling what degree of perfection you will attain in the art of gardening, for truly no one will deny it is an art.

Milo Miloradovich

Contents

18   *Contents*

Growing and Using Herbs and Spices

Herbs

in a Small Garden

Many of the designs of our modern herb gardens are variations and sometimes copies of the traditional herb gardens of antiquity. However, it isn't necessary to have an elaborate plan or a traditional design in order to enjoy the many pleasures of herb gardening.

A simple row of fragrant herbs along a garden walk or a few varieties planted in between the rows of a vegetable garden can prove to be a really satisfactory beginning. If the herbs are grown in rows in the vegetable garden, very little space is required. Generally speaking, only a few feet of the annuals and but five or six plants of the selected perennials will supply generously the needs of the average family.

The design and plan of your herb garden, like that of any other garden, can be one of personal preference according to the space you may have to devote to the planting. If the garden space is limited, a small plot not more than 4 feet square can be a source of unpretentious enjoyment. An oblong or an irregularly shaped garden space not more than a few feet wide and approximately 6 feet long will be large enough to grow a sufficient supply of savory herbs for the entire family to enjoy.

In other words, an herb garden may be planted in practically any part of the available space where there is well-drained soil. The selected group of herbs may be planted to harmonize with any of the surrounding landscape, and one need not necessarily follow a traditional design. If desired, the herb bed may be raised somewhat above the level of the surroundings by filling in the bed with extra soil. The edges and border of the design may be kept neat and firm very easily by sinking a metal or wooden boundary into the ground about 2 inches deep. It is best to keep the perennials separate from the other herbs so they will not be disturbed by the planting of the annuals.

DIVERSITY OF DESIGN

Designs in triangles, ovals, and circles lend themselves to herb planting if one prefers them to the squares and oblongs. The planning of the design can give as much pleasure as the charting of a flower garden. In many instances the herb garden is infinitely more simple. The various degrees of the colors of the herb foliage can be used to create a design within a design. The gray-greens, the blue-greens, the deep greens, the purplegreens, and the light greens may be planted in such a way as to create exquisite contrasts. For example, the vivid deep green foliage of the humble yet beautiful curly parsley makes a perfect border for a gray-green center of rosemary, sage, tarragon, and thyme.

There are several beautifully designed herb gardens in our parks and botanical gardens. Sketches of two such modern designs are included in this book. As an example of what an herb garden can be without benefit of a design, I have sketched the herb garden which I knew as a child. It had no formal planning, but the herbs which grew in that simple oblong space were a source of constant and fragrant delight. It amply supplied aromatic culinary herbs for our family and for several neighbors. Like the herb gardens in colonial times, it was as near the kitchen door as it was possible to have it. Anyone could run out to pinch off a sprig of thyme or a few leaves of rosemary and chervil to add to the deliciousness of a marvelous roast or a tasty, savory stuffing.

If there is no available separate space in your garden for herbs only, it still will be possible for you to grow a few of them. A small border of the shorter, bushy herbs may be planted along a pathway or against a background of shrubs where there is a sunny exposure. The herbs will add not only fragrance but real beauty to the surroundings. Or a few plants may be tucked into an extra crevice in the rock garden or used as a border for an already thriving flower bed.

Naturally, the herbs chosen for a rock garden will include the shorter spreading herbs such as camomile, winter savory, and a variety or two of the trailing thymes. All these require little care and will thrive in the cracks and crevices and gaily add their charm to the colorful combination of the other plants. As an easy reference to assist you in choosing various herbs adapted for planting in particular places in the garden, the herbs have each been classified and assembled into such lists at the end of this chapter.

ADAPTABILITY OF HERBS

A great variety of the fragrant herbs will grow in practically all garden soils which are suitable for growing vegetables. In fact, many of them will thrive better in a poorer soil which is well drained. When the soil is too rich, the growth is apt to result in a heavy, luxuriant foliage rather than developing foliage filled with volatile oil which gives the richer, more aromatic flavor. Since most of the savory herbs will grow under a wide range of different climates and soil conditions, cultivating suggestions are given in the later chapters of this volume under each specific herb. The spices adaptable to cultivation in our hemisphere are also included.

The seed and young seedlings of the many fragrant herbs may be obtained from a goodly number of established herb gardens, local seedsmen, and nurseries all over the country. See also the listing at the back of this book: Where Fragrant Herb Plants and Seed May Be Purchased. Once your own garden is started, it is quite simple to enlarge it as you wish. Since many of the herbs are perennials, you will have root divisions not only for yourself but for all your friends and neighbors as well.

SUGGESTIONS FOR A FIRST HERB GARDEN

Among the especially delightful and useful herbs which may be selected as starters in a small garden are sweet basil, chervil,

chives, dill, fennel, sweet marjoram, one or two of the scented
mints, parsley, lemon verbena, rose geranium, sage, summer
savory, tarragon, and thyme.

Herb gardens, like other gardens, reflect the taste and personality of the owner and the gardener, and no two gardens can
ever be quite alike. Since any or all of the annuals, biennials,
and perennials on the following lists are readily and easily
grown, one's own choice may be made from among those
herbs whose colors and fragrances are personal favorites. It is
much more exciting to have complete success with but five or
six herbs at first. Then as one learns what satisfactory and
fascinating little plants they can be, additional varieties may
be added to the garden without difficulty and with genuine enthusiasm.

PLANT DISEASES—NOT FREQUENT

The majority of the popular culinary herbs are free from
troublesome plant diseases, especially when they are grown in
small quantities, under the right conditions, and are never over-
crowded. Should rust occasionally turn the leaves of the mints,
tarragon, or thyme, this is readily counteracted by spraying
them with sulphur and burning all the old stems and plants.
Rust rarely attacks sweet marjoram, summer savory, sage, or
rosemary, and never troubles chives, dill, chervil, parsley, water
cress, or the sweet basils. In fact, disease is unusual with most
of the culinary herbs, and this is another reason they can be so
satisfactory for the gardener.

In certain regions and under unusually dry weather conditions, sage may be attacked by a small mite or lace bug. However, the disease seldom causes serious damage and a spray of
yellow soap suds will control it. The culinary herbs require a
minimum of watching and are usually healthy. Should a serious disease attack any of the plants, it is best to treat them as
recommended by the county agent or the state agricultural
experiment station, since local climate and soil conditions
differ. If you are fortunate enough to be near a local herb
gardener, he or she will gladly share and exchange herb-grow-
ing experiences with you. In herb gardening in the Pacific
Northwest, I remember having no trouble whatsoever with
plant diseases.

HERBS EASILY GROWN IN A SMALL GARDEN

Annuals

Basil, Purple	Chervil	Lavender, English
Basil, Sweet	Dill	Marjoram, Sweet
Borage	Fennel, Sweet	Savory, Summer

Biennials

Angelica	Caraway	Parsley

Perennials

Bergamot, Wild	Peppermint
Burnet	Rose Geranium
Camomile	Rosemary
Catnip	Rue
Chives	Sage, Garden
Horehound	Savory, Winter
Lovage	Sorrel
Mint, Apple	Spearmint
Mint, Curly	Tarragon, French
Mint, Orange	Thyme, English
Parsley, when kept from	Thyme, Lemon
seeding	Verbena, Lemon

SELECTING CULINARY HERBS FOR INDIVIDUAL GARDENS

Foliage colors for creating designs—dominant shades

BLUE-GREEN FOLIAGE

Basil, Dwarf	Rue
Dill	Lavender, English

GRAY-GREEN FOLIAGE

Catnip	Mint, Apple
Corn Salad	Orégano
Lavender, French	Rosemary
Lavender, Spike	Sage
Marjorams	Thyme, English

DEEP GREEN FOLIAGE

Basil, Sweet
Burnet
Chervil
Chives
Horseradish
Hyssop
Leek

Marigold
Parsley, Curly
Peppermint, Black
Savory, Summer
Tansy
Tarragon, French
Water Cress

LIGHT GREEN FOLIAGE

Angelica
Balm, Lemon
Costmary
Fennel
Lovage

Peppermint, White
Nasturtium
Parsley, Fern-leaved
Poppy
Sorrel

PURPLE-GREEN FOLIAGE

Basil, Purple

Mint, Orange

Blossom colors for grouping—dominant shades

PALE TO DEEP BLUE

Borage
Catnip
Corn Salad

Hyssop, Blue
Lavender, True
Rosemary

CRIMSON

Bergamot, Red
Ginger

Sage, Pineapple
Thyme, Trailing

GREENISH-YELLOW

Lovage

MAUVE TO PURPLE

Bergamot Mint
Catnip
Cumin
Lavender, Spike

Mints
Sage, Garden
Savory, Winter
Thyme, Woolly

PALE TO DEEP PINK

Burnet
Coriander
Hyssop, Pink

Savory, Summer
Savory, Winter

WHITE

Angelica
Burnet
Camomile
Chervil
Cumin
Horehound

Hyssop, White
Marjoram, Sweet
Poppy, White
Sage, White
Thyme, White
Woodruff, Sweet

YELLOWISH-WHITE

Anise
Caraway

Tarragon, French

YELLOWS TO ORANGE

Balm, Lemon
Costmary
Dill
Fennel, Sweet
Marigold

Mustard
Saffron, True
Tansy
Turmeric

For planting in shady or partially shady places

ANNUAL

Chervil

BIENNIAL

Angelica
Parsley (Perennial when kept from seeding)

PERENNIALS

Balm, Lemon
Burnet, Garden
Costmary

Mints
Tarragon, French
Thyme, Lemon
Woodruff, Sweet

For planting in sunny places

ANNUALS

Anise
Borage
Camomile, German
Coriander
Dill

Fennel, Sweet
Marjoram, Sweet
Orégano
Savory, Summer
Sesame

BIENNIALS

Caraway

Parsley

PERENNIALS

Bergamot	Mints
Burnet, Garden	Parsley
Camomile, Roman	Rosemary
Catnip	Sage, Garden
Chives	Savory, Winter
Horehound	Sorrel, Garden
Lavenders	Tarragon, French
Lovage	Thymes

For attracting honeybees

Balm, Lemon	Lavenders
Basil, Sweet	Marigold
Bergamot, Red	Marjoram, Sweet
Borage	Orégano
Camomile	Rosemary
Catnip	Sage
Fennel, Sweet	Savory, Winter
Hyssop	Thymes

As hedges and back borders

Angelica	Hyssop	Rosemary
Bergamot	Lovage	Sage, Pineapple
Costmary	Orégano	Tansy

As edges and low borders

Basil, Dwarf	Chives	Savory, Winter
Camomile	Parsley, Curly	Thyme, English

In rock gardens

Balm, Bee	
Borage	Savory, Winter
Lavender, English*	Thyme, Wild
Marjoram, Sweet	Woodruff, Sweet

As ground carpets

Camomile, Roman	Thyme, Wild
Thyme, Lemon	Woodruff, Sweet

*Especially atop and against a stone wall.

Two variations of the traditional herb garden

**SECTION OF HERB GARDEN OF THE NEW YORK
BOTANICAL GARDENS PLANTED BY THE NEW YORK
UNIT OF THE HERB SOCIETY OF AMERICA**

1. Rosmarinus officinalis
2. Nepeta Mussinii
3. Teucrium marum
4. Lavandula officinalis "Munstead"
5. Satureia montana
6. Comptonia peregrina
7. Inula Helenium
8. Myrrhis odorata
9. Viola odorata
10. Primula veris
11. Marrubium candidissimum
12. Salvia pratensis
13. Salvia pratensis
14. Cassia marilandica
15. Monarda didyma
16. Digitalis ambigua
17. Monarda didyma
18. Monarda didyma (red)
19. Campanula rapunculoides
20. Sanguisorba minor
21. Thymus vulgaris
22. Stachys officinalis
23. Salvia officinalis
24. Chrysanthemum Parthenium
25. Hyssopus officinalis (pink)
26. Lavandula o. "Munstead"
27. Allium Moly
28. Artemisia albula "Silver King"
29. Artemisia Abrotanum
30. Rosmarinus officinalis
31. Origanum dictamnus
32. Sanguisorba canadensis
33. Dianthus "Old Spice"
34. Dictamnus albus
35. Hyssopus officinalis (pink)
36. Lavendula o. "Munstead"
37. Crocus sativus
38. Thymus vulgaris
39. Hyssopus officinalis (blue)
40. Rosa "Kazanlik" (Rosa damascena trigintipetalia)
41. Rumex scutatus
42. Allium flavum
43. Thymus vulgaris
44. Hyssopus officinalis (white)
45. Angelica Archangelica
46. Salvia officinalis
47. Iris Germanica florentina
48. Artemisia Purshiana
49. Micromeria rupestris
50. Lavandula officinalis
51. Fragaria vesca alba
52. Santolina Chamaecyparissus
53. Thymus vulgaris

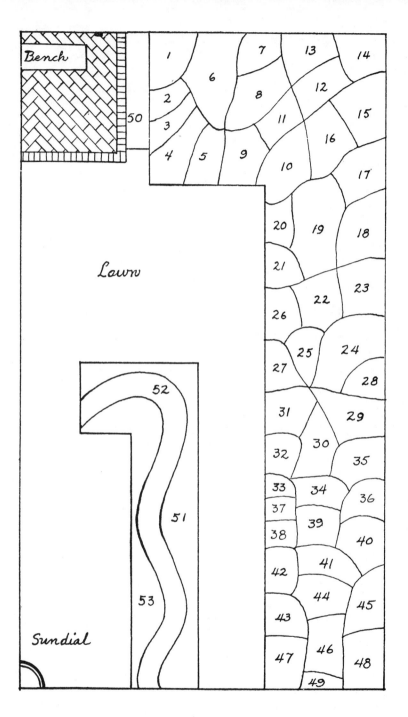

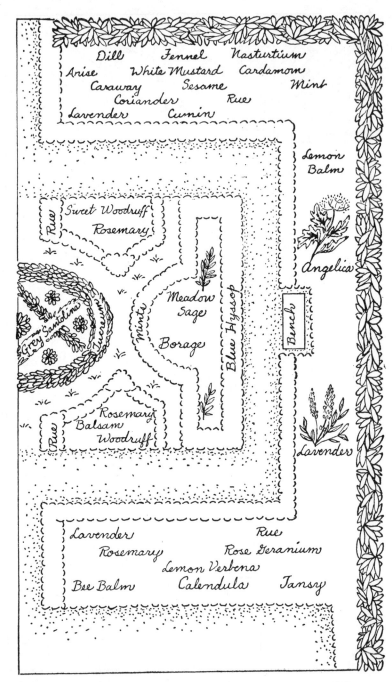

Dill   Fennel   Nasturtium
Anise   White Mustard   Cardamom
   Caraway   Sesame   Mint
    Coriander   Rue
Lavender   Cumin

Lemon Balm

Angelica

Rue Sweet Woodruff
   Rosemary

Grey Santolina

Lavender

Tarragon

Mints

Meadow Sage

Borage

Blue Hyssop

Bench

Rue Rosemary
Balsam
  Woodruff

Lavender

Lavender   Rue
  Rosemary   Rose Geranium
    Lemon Verbena
Bee Balm   Calendula   Tansy

**WESTERN RESERVE HERB SOCIETY'S HERB GARDEN
IN WADE PARK, CLEVELAND, OHIO**

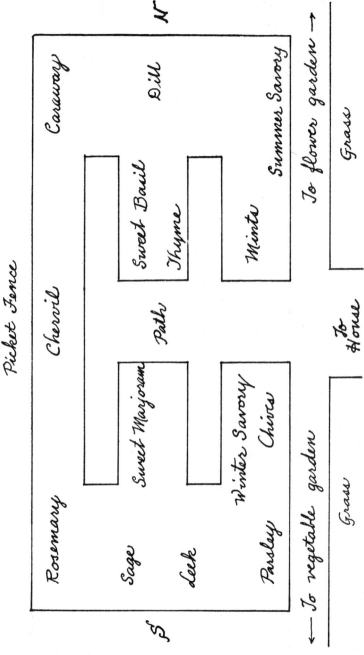

AUTHOR'S HERB GARDEN IN SPOKANE, WASHINGTON

CHAPTER TWO

Herbs Indoors in a Window Box

Several of the savory herbs may be easily grown indoors, either during the winter months or all year, so that one may have the pleasure of using fresh herbs at all times.

Since the annuals mature their seed and then die at the end of the growing season, it is best to plan to have new seedlings in the fall ready to bring indoors. The seed should be planted outdoors sufficiently early in the autumn so the tiny seedlings will be ready for indoor transplanting just before the frost.

The perennials will give the best results if the window-box plants are started from root cuttings or divisions rather than attempting to bring the old plants indoors. If there is no outdoor garden and you are starting your window box from scratch, the seedlings may be purchased from an herb garden or local nursery.

The herb window box is a lovely thing, and it doesn't necessarily have to stand along the kitchen window sill either. Undoubtedly there will be a rose geranium or two and perhaps some sweet marjoram and thyme with the ever-popular parsley, chives, and mints. These decorative herbs will add attractiveness and fragrant aroma to any room in the house.

Standard window boxes which can be kept well drained are the best. However, if boxes with such drainage structure are not procurable, any window box with a thick layer of rocks and stones placed on the bottom will be all right. Then the surplus moisture will lie below the soil. The box should be placed in a sunny window where the temperature can be kept even and where the box can be turned occasionally so that both sides get plenty of sun.

If one prefers only a pot or two of herbs, the 4-inch pots are the best size. Place them on trays at least 2 or 3 inches deep with a layer of stones or broken pot pieces spread thickly along the bottom of the trays. This allows for good drainage. Water should be kept in the trays at all times, but it should not touch the pots. The plants should be watered frequently from the top and then soaked about every ten days by letting the pots stand in water for an hour or more.

By following the general rules of caring for the average house plant, many varieties of herbs may be successfully grown indoors. Simply give them plenty of light, moisture, and fresh air which is neither too hot nor too dry.

Prepared potting soil may be purchased. If so, have a goodly portion of sand mixed with it, otherwise it will be too rich for most herbs. When regular loam is used, mix three parts of it with one part sand and one part fertilizer.

Several of the tall herbs listed, such as dill, fennel, and rosemary, become dwarfed when planted indoors in window boxes and pots; and they make beautiful house plants.

ANNUALS

Basil, Sweet
Chervil
Dill
Fennel, Sweet
Marjoram, Sweet
Savory, Summer

BIENNIALS

Parsley

PERENNIALS

Balm, Lemon
Chives
Mint, Apple
Mint, Orange
Parsley, when kept
  from seeding
Peppermint
Rose Geranium
Rosemary
Sage
Savory, Winter
Tarragon, French
Thyme, Garden
Thyme, Lemon
Verbena, Lemon

CHAPTER THREE

Developing Seedlings for Early Transplanting

Everyone with an understanding of a few of the fundamental rules of good gardening may have complete success in growing herbs. It needs but a little time and patience in which to become familiar with the specific idiosyncrasies and natures of the individual species. Particular cultivation suggestions are given later in those chapters devoted to each herb and spice.

There are many of the garden herbs which do not thrive if they are transplanted. These herbs, therefore, should be planted only out of doors, either in the autumn or the early spring, as the case may be. Then they may remain undisturbed in their designated places in the garden. See also names of herbs.

Moreover, when one wishes to start seed indoors in pots or small seedbeds, the same fundamentals of good planting should be observed as one uses in the out-of-doors. One of the first and perhaps most important essentials is to make certain that only fresh, good seed are used. Next, be sure that the soil is a light, non-acid, sandy mixture which is absolutely sterile. A good, tested combination is approximately ⅓ sand, ⅓ compost, and ⅓ loam. A simple way to sterilize the soil is by pouring boiling water through it.

Until the seed germinate, the soil should be kept moist and the pots or seedbeds covered with paper or thin glass. After germination, care should be taken not to give the seedlings too much water and to keep the soil well drained at all times. See also Chapter Two, "Herbs Indoors in a Window Box."

SEEDLINGS IN COLD FRAMES

Unless the gardener wishes to cultivate herbs in large commercial quantities, he or she need not be too concerned about the artificially heated outdoor bed and the cold frame. However, since there may be some readers who may wish to rush the season by developing seedlings for early transplanting, a few suggestions on cold frames are given.

The purpose of the cold-frame planting is to produce strong, healthy plants which can stand transplanting early in the season into the open garden without having their natural growth checked by the change. The cold frame acts as a protection against the cold winds. The sash or canvas or muslin cover enables the gardener to regulate the amount of air and sunlight which the young seedlings need for their best development.

How to construct a cold frame

A frame for a small bed 3 by 6 feet is not difficult to construct. It should be located on level ground where there will be no danger of flooding during a heavy rainstorm. Build the frame, if possible, near or against the south side of a building where it will be well protected. Also place it conveniently near the spot where the plants can be given frequent attention when necessary.

The framework of boards is built on top of the ground and the boards nailed to stakes driven into the ground. The boards should be at least 1 inch thick, 12 inches wide, and of either cypress or good hard white pine. Use two boards for the back, which should be the north side of the frame, and one board, 1 foot high, for the front (or south) side of the frame.

Crosspieces of two-by-fours nailed over the top will support the glass sash or the heavy muslin or canvas covering, whichever type the climatic conditions require. Along the Atlantic Coast, where both the early spring and the late fall climate is mild, the heavy canvas covering is sufficient. If there should be a short period of unusually cold weather, the bed may be further protected by covering the canvas top of the cold frame with a thin layer of straw. When the temperature rises, the straw may be swept off easily.

In the colder climates the glass sash covering is required for the cold frame. There are several ready-made economical types of sashes on the market. However, there is a growing tendency to develop seedlings in modern beautifully designed and electrically heated greenhouses.

In the Southern regions, where the climate is regularly mild, a ridgepole supported on stakes 30 inches high may be run through the center of the cold-frame bed. Light canvas or muslin is used as a cover and may be fastened to the ridgepole by tacking it down. A thin strip of wood, such as plasterers' lath, laid on the canvas or muslin before tacking, will protect it from tearing. The edges of the canvas may be fastened to the crosspieces and readily rolled up on them when the plant beds are ventilated.

Ventilating the cold frame

When ventilating the cold frame, care should be taken to roll back the canvas covering or raise the sash on the side opposite the direction from which the wind is blowing. Toward the end of the growing season of the young seedlings, the coverings may be kept partly open at all times. Finally, they should be removed completely so the plants will adapt themselves to the outside weather conditions.

TRANSPLANTING SEEDLINGS INTO THE OPEN GARDEN

When seedlings are ready for transplanting, a cube of earth should be carried with them to the transplanting plot. If one wishes the herb to develop a luxuriant leafy growth, a richer, more fertilized soil may be used. However, at all times the soil must be kept alkaline. If the soil needs lime, this should be dug into the soil a week or two before any fertilizer has been added, except when using wood ashes. This fertilizer may be added at any time.

If the herb is to be used for its fragrance and aromatic flavor, the plant will develop a greater amount of the necessary essential oil which gives this flavor if the soil is definitely on the poorer side.

WATERING THE YOUNG PLANTS

During cloudy weather, the plants will require less water than during the bright sunny days. Careful attention at all times to both watering and ventilation will prevent any loss of young seedlings through damping off. Also water the seedlings only when the covers may be opened safely without danger of chilling the plants. As the growing season ends, less water should be given to the seedlings, since this helps them in the tempering process of becoming accustomed to the outdoor conditions.

CHAPTER FOUR

Culinary Herbs
Adapted to Growing
in Various
Geographical Localities

EASTERN UNITED STATES, CANADA, ENGLAND, AND THE CONTINENT

Culinary herbs which thrive in the cold, cool, and temperate zones and climates such as are found in the Eastern United States, Canada, England, and the Continent. Especially in the states of Connecticut, Delaware, Maine, Maryland, Massachusetts, New Hampshire, New Jersey, New York, Pennsylvania, Rhode Island, and Vermont; also in Manitoba, New Brunswick, Newfoundland, Nova Scotia, Ontario, and Quebec, Canada. See also name of each herb.

Angelica	Chives	Lavender, Spike
Balm, Lemon	Coriander	Leek
Basil, Sweet	Corn Salad	Lovage
Bergamot, Wild	Cress, Land	Marigold
Borage	Cumin	Marjoram, Sweet
Burnet	Dill	Mints
Camomile	Fennel	Mustard
Caraway	Garlic	Orégano
Catnip	Horehound	Parsley
Celery	Horseradish	Peppers
Chervil	Hyssop	Poppy

Rose Geranium	Savory, Summer	Thyme
Rosemary	Savory, Winter	Verbena, Lemon
Rue	Sorrel	Water Cress
Saffron	Tansy	Woodruff
Sage	Tarragon, French	

MIDDLE WESTERN UNITED STATES

Culinary herbs which thrive in the cold, cool, and temperate zones and climates such as are found in the states of the Middle West. Especially those states of Illinois, Indiana, Iowa, Kansas, Michigan, Missouri, Nebraska, and Ohio. Also Arkansas and Oklahoma. See also name of each herb.

Angelica	Dill	Poppy
Balm, Lemon	Fennel	Rose Geranium
Basil, Sweet	Garlic	Rosemary
Bergamot, Wild	Horehound	Rue
Borage	Horseradish	Saffron
Burnet	Hyssop	Sage
Camomile	Lavender, English	Savory, Summer
Caraway	Lavender, Spike	Savory, Winter
Catnip	Leek	Sesame
Celery	Lovage	Sorrel
Chervil	Marigold	Tansy
Chives	Marjoram, Sweet	Tarragon, French
Coriander	Mints	Thyme
Corn Salad	Mustard	Verbena, Lemon
Cress, Land	Orégano	Water Cress
Cumin	Parsley	Woodruff, Sweet
	Peppers	

SOUTHERN UNITED STATES AND SOUTHERN EUROPE

Culinary herbs which thrive in the temperate, warm, and hot zones and climates of the Southern United States and southern Europe. Especially those states of Alabama, Florida, Georgia, Kentucky, Louisiana, Mississippi, North Carolina, South Carolina, Tennessee, Virginia, and West Virginia. See also name of each herb.

Anise	Dill	Poppy
Balm, Lemon	Fennel	Rose Geranium
Basil, Sweet	Garlic	Rosemary
Bay or True Laurel	Ginger, Florida	Rue
Bergamot	Ginger, Jamaica	Saffron
Borage	Horehound	Sage
Burnet	Hyssop	Savory, Summer
Camomile	Lavender	Savory, Winter
Caraway	Leek	Sesame
Catnip	Lovage	Shallots
Celery	Marigold	Sorrel
Chervil	Marjoram, Sweet	Tansy
Chives	Mints	Tarragon, French
Coriander	Mustard	Thyme
Corn Salad	Orégano	Verbena, Lemon
Cress, Land	Parsley	Water Cress
Cumin	Peppers	Woodruff, Sweet

SOUTHWESTERN UNITED STATES AND MEXICO

Culinary herbs which thrive in the cool, temperate, and warm zones of the Southwestern United States. Especially those states of Arizona, California, New Mexico, Texas, and in Mexico. These herbs also thrive in Colorado, Nevada, and Utah. See also name of each herb.

Balm, Lemon	Dill	Rose Geranium
Basil, Sweet	Fennel, Sweet	Rosemary
Bergamot, Wild	Garlic	Rue
Borage	Horehound	Saffron
Burnet	Hyssop	Sage
Camomile	Lavender, Spike	Savory, Summer
Caraway	Leek	Savory, Winter
Catnip	Lovage	Sesame
Celery	Marigold	Tansy
Chervil	Marjoram, Sweet	Sorrel
Chives	Mints	Tarragon, French
Coriander	Mustard Seed	Thyme
Corn Salad	Orégano	Verbena, Lemon
Cress, Land	Parsley	Water Cress
Cumin	Peppers	Woodruff, Sweet
	Poppy	

WESTERN AND NORTHWESTERN UNITED STATES AND CANADA

Culinary herbs which thrive in the cold, cool, and temperate zones and climates of the Western and Northwestern United States and Canada. Especially those states of Idaho, Montana, North Dakota, Oregon, South Dakota, Washington, Wisconsin, Wyoming, and the southern part of the Territory of Alaska; also Alberta, British Columbia, Saskatchewan, and the southern part of the Yukon in Canada. See also name of each herb.

Balm, Lemon	Garlic	Poppy
Basil, Sweet	Horehound	Rose Geranium
Bergamot, Wild	Horseradish	Rosemary
Borage	Hyssop	Rue
Burnet	Lavender, Spike	Saffron
Camomile	Leek	Sage
Caraway	Lovage	Savory, Summer
Catnip	Marigold	Savory, Winter
Celery	Marjoram, Sweet	Sorrel
Chives	Mints	Tarragon, French
Corn Salad	Mustard Seed	Thyme
Cress, Land	Orégano	Verbena, Lemon
Cumin	Parsley	Water Cress
Dill	Peppers	Woodruff, Sweet
Fennel, Sweet		

CHAPTER FIVE

Drying

Herbs

The flavor of the savory herbs is in the essential oils contained in the tiny glands in leaves, fruits, and seed of the plants. The fresh flavor is better and lasts longer if the herbs are harvested when the plants first begin to blossom, for at that time the oil content is at its highest. Fresh flavor is also dependent upon the herbs being carefully dried and stored.

When cutting the fresh, young leaves for use at any time during the season, it is best to gather them in the early morning of a warm, sunny day just as the last drops of dew are evaporating.

When herbs are cut for winter use, they should be harvested at the time when the plants first begin to flower. Then they should be dried as rapidly as possible in a shady, or dark, well-ventilated place. All the tender leaf herbs such as basil, costmary, lemon balm, the mints, and tarragon should be dried quickly and away from all sunlight so they may retain their natural colors. Drying small quantities of herbs in any dark, well-ventilated room will be even more ideal than drying them in an outdoor spot, for then it is easier to keep the herbs free from dust particles.

It is always wise to allow a few plants among the annual varieties to flower fully and mature seed for planting each successive year. When the herbs are grown for the seed crop, the umbels and pods should be harvested just as they mature and when their color changes from green to a brown or gray.

45

Specific suggestions on harvesting seed are given later in this chapter.

Both leaves and seed should be packed in suitable containers which will prevent loss of color and delicate flavor. Opaque plastic or glass, or glass painted black, and metal are the best; but cardboard containers which can be as tightly sealed as the glass, plastic, or metal ones will be satisfactory. If opaque containers or jars are not available, the herbs may be stored in clear·glass if they are kept in a dark room to prevent bleaching by the light.

General rules on when and how to cut and prepare annuals and perennials for drying are given here, as well as specific ones for the handling and drying of bunches of herbs, flower heads, leaves, petals, roots, and seed.

CUTTING AND PREPARING

Cut just as buds open into full blossom.
Cut on a sunny morning, after the dew is off the leaves and before the sun is high.
Cut annuals within 4 inches of the ground.
Cut perennials with side branches and stems ⅔ of the length of the stalks.
Quickly rinse off all earth and dirt which may cling to lower leaves.
Spread stalks on tray or screen.
Remove all yellow, rusty, decayed leaves; also all coarse ends and leaves.

DRYING BUNCHES OF HERBS

Tie leafy stems in bunches.
Label each variety carefully.
Hang bunches on a cord or line strung in a dry, airy attic or in the shade out of doors.
Lay sheet on floor or earth to catch all leaves which fall.
Leaves must be crackly and thoroughly dried; this usually takes about 4 days.
Take each bunch down carefully.
Lay each variety in a separate basket.
Strip leaves off by hand; wearing an old cotton glove will protect the fingers.

Keep whole leaves for tea and other uses as desired.

Rub other leaves through coarse sieve to powder them.

Small herbs with tiny leaves and stems need not be stripped but may be put through a meat grinder, using a coarse blade or wheel.

Store in large, clear container placed in dark room and watch herbs for a week. If moisture appears inside, pour them out and dry for 3 or 4 more days.

Store in small opaque containers, tightly corked or sealed.

DRYING FLOWER HEADS

Cut in early morning, when dew is evaporated. ·

Cut off heads when blossoms are opened fully.

Spread heads on cheesecloth-covered screen or tray placed in a shady, airy spot, or in a dry, warm, clean attic.

When thoroughly dry, strip heads from stalks by hand.

Store in clear container in cool, dark room; watch one week for moisture.

Redry if necessary.

Store in small, opaque containers, tightly corked or sealed.

DRYING LEAVES

Strip fresh, perfect leaves from stalks.

Spread a thin layer of leaves on cheesecloth-covered screen or tray in a shady spot.

Place so that air circulates under as well as over screen.

Gently turn leaves once a day.

If drying out of doors, bring indoors every night before dew falls.

Leaves should be dry in 3 or 4 days.

Store in clear containers in dark room; watch one week for moisture.

Store in small, opaque containers, tightly corked or sealed.

DRYING PETALS

Cut in early morning, when dew is evaporated.

Cut off heads when flowers are opened fully.

Remove florets by hand.

Spread carefully on cheesecloth-covered screen so petals do not touch.

Place screen in shady spot and where air may circulate under as well as over petals.

A warm, airy room is best for drying petals.

When thoroughly dried, store in tightly covered containers; watch for one week. If moisture appears inside, pour out and dry another day or two.

Finally store in opaque containers, tightly corked or sealed.

See also Harvesting Saffron stigmas, pages 169–70.

DRYING ROOTS

Roots such as angelica and lovage are dug in the same way as root vegetables.

Place on wire screen.

Wash roots thoroughly with a hose.

Scrape roots, if necessary, to remove all earth and dirt.

Slice roots or split lengthwise, as desired.

Spread in thin layers on a wire screen placed in a dry, shady spot.

Bring indoors every night before dew falls.

Carefully turn slices 2 or 3 times each week so they may dry evenly on all sides.

When the roots are partially dry, the screen may be placed in a warm oven at very low heat with the door left open; this will hasten the drying.

Drying takes from 3 to 6 weeks.

If the slice breaks with a snap when tested or broken, it is dry and ready to be stored.

Place in opaque containers which may be tightly sealed.

DRYING SEED

On a dry hot day cut off seed heads when the stalks look dry and the umbels are brown or gray.

Easiest way is to gather them in a basket lined with cheesecloth; hold the basket under the umbels or seed pods as they are cut from the stems.

Spread seed heads or pods in a thin layer on a heavy cloth or cheesecloth-covered tray placed in a warm, dry spot.

Occasionally turn or stir *pods* gently for 5 or 6 days.

Carefully rub dried pods through the palms of the hands.

If done while there is a breeze, the chaff will blow away.

Spread seed on cheesecloth-covered screen placed in a warm, dry spot.

Turn *seed* gently once or twice a day for at least a week.

When dry, store in clear containers placed in dark room; watch for 2 weeks. If moisture appears, pour out; dry several days longer.

Store in opaque containers, tightly corked or sealed.

CHAPTER SIX

Quick-Freezing

and Preserving

Fresh Herbs

There are many of us to whom the words "preserving" and "salting down" bring back memories of luscious canned fruits and vegetables, or tangy relishes and chowchow. We think of the garden-fresh cucumbers and crisp cabbages which were salted in brine to turn them into those delicious-tasting pickles and sauerkraut.

Sometimes, too, our grandmothers minced fresh herbs and preserved them in butter, or salted down the whole herb with its tender stems. Then, in the deep of winter, a sprig of tarragon or thyme was taken from the crock to be rinsed in cold running water before being minced and used to flavor a succulent roast chicken, or as the extra seasoning for a special stuffing.

Such culinary procedures may sound strange to our modern ears, but it was once considered a gourmet's privilege and delight to have home-preserved or salted-down herbs from one's own garden for use in the kitchen when ice and snow covered even the hardiest perennials. Even today there are still some homemakers who will take the time and use infinite patience to salt down freshly minced herbs or sprigs of dill and parsley and basil. But for those whose time is more limited and whose home equipment includes a deep freeze, there is the convenient delight of having fresh, quick-frozen herbs.

It was Mrs. Gertrude B. Foster, the imaginative owner of the Laurel Hill Herb Farm in Falls Village, Connecticut, who began experimenting with herbs and discovered which specific herbs would retain their true flavors when quick-frozen. Mrs. Foster, who is also editor of *The Herb Grower Magazine,* is a pioneer in the quick-freezing of herbs. She has spent more than four years in testing and developing a successful quick-freezing procedure for herbs so that you and I might have them fragrant, flavorful, and garden-fresh from the deep freeze in the middle of the coldest winter.

SELECTING HERBS FOR QUICK-FREEZING

The herbs which retain their full summertime flavor, according to the experiments and records, are *sweet basil, salad burnet, chervil, chives, dill, fennel, lovage, sweet marjoram, spearmint, parsley, sage, sorrel, French tarragon,* and *thyme.* Only the sorrel herb needs special handling because the tender leaves break apart and become very slippery in the boiling water used for blanching. Therefore, sorrel leaves should be placed in a wire basket after the heavy stems and midribs have been removed. The basket makes the handling of them easier and prevents them from floating around in the water. The sorrel leaves lose their color and turn brown in the process, but the flavor remains fresh and natural.

INSTRUCTIONS FOR QUICK-FREEZING

The process is as simple as freezing spinach or other greens. Speed in working and lightness of touch are the two most important requisites for successful quick-freezing. Purchase some cellophane bags which can be heat-sealed, and buy some small wax cartons, either the half-pint or the pint size. The only other equipment necessary is a large pan filled with boiling water, ready for blanching, and another pan filled with ice water for rapid cooling and thorough chilling.

Naturally the entire crispness cannot be restored after the blanching, but the quick-frozen herbs may be used in all the ways in which the fresh ones are used, except as garnishes. In iced drinks and infusions, the flavor is superb; and the quick-frozen herbs may be crushed or finely minced just as easily as the fresh ones.

These simple rules will make the quick-freezing of herbs a real joy and a delightful success:

Gather herbs in the early morning of a sunny day before the warmth of the air has dried all the dew.

Cut tender tops with sufficient stems to tie the herbs in small bunches.

If necessary, wash in cold running water; dry on absorbent paper.

Separate all clean sprigs.

Arrange sprigs of herbs singly or in combinations just as they will be used in recipes. (Combinations save time and work.)

Knot a loop of thread about stems so herbs may be dipped without scalding fingers.

Keep water in kettle at boiling point, for blanching.

Dip only few herbs at a time; that is, enough for a recipe.

Quickly *dip completely under boiling water* 1 minute. (Sweet basil turns black if steam hits leaves before they are under water.)

Plunge tied sprigs into ice water for 2 minutes or until thoroughly chilled; or

Hold under very cold running water until herbs are thoroughly chilled.

Drain leaves of excess water.

Place in cellophane bags which can be heat-sealed.

Enclose several bags in small wax carton (½-pint or 1-pint size).

Label cartons to make later selection easy.

Place in deep freeze until ready to use.

USING QUICK-FROZEN HERBS

When ready to use, transfer herbs from deep freeze to refrigerator.

Thaw herbs at room temperature.

Use immediately after thawing.

Never refreeze.

If leaves are left over, place in glass jar; cover with wine vinegar; use for salad dressings.

HERB BLENDS

As mentioned previously, preparing combinations of herbs at the time of freezing them makes for efficiency and economy when they are taken from the deep freeze for use. One then has an herb blend immediately ready without opening several different containers. For example, favorite combinations may be prepared and marked for soups, others for salads, and still others for roasts and herb stuffings. One may combine chervil and rosemary for poultry; chervil and tarragon for salads; or thyme and sweet marjoram for use in seasoning veal. See also "Herb Blends and Bouquets" in author's *The Art of Cooking with Herbs and Spices*.

PRESERVING FRESH HERBS IN SALT

There are many herb enthusiasts who still enjoy using the old-fashioned method our grandmothers used to preserve the fresh color and flavor of the culinary herbs by salting them down. This method also takes real patience, as do all good things, but the reward is well worth the effort.

The majority of culinary herbs which may be salted down will retain much of their natural color as well as their garden-fresh flavor. The basic recipe which I have given here was a favorite of my mother. Since deep freezes were unknown quantities in those days, the crocks or jars were kept in the cellar. There, whenever the covers of the crocks were lifted, the aroma of the herbs was mouth-watering, especially that of the dill. I always loved to go down to the cellar to bring up crisp, luscious dill pickles just before mealtimes. On a cold winter's evening, the crunching of a juicy dill pickle on the way up the stairs was my youthful idea of an *apéritif* without equal.

The herbs most satisfactory and especially adapted to the old-fashioned method of preserving in salt are the whole sprigs of sweet basil, chervil, dill, and similar herbs which are used for seasoning soups, sauces, and chowders.

The secret of many an unusually delicious sauce is in the use of either the salted-down or the quick-frozen garden-fresh herbs. There is a little Italian restaurant down on Grand Street in New York, called Nuova Napoli, which brings people from as far away as Chicago to eat there because of a superb sweet-basil tomato sauce. This sauce's unique flavor is the result of the use of the garden-fresh, salted-down *basilico,* sweet basil, which Tony, the chef, uses with such culinary art. Very proudly he told me that he selects the fresh sweet basil and salts it down himself for the exclusive use in his restaurant.

Whether you choose the quick-freezing method of preserving fresh herbs or use the old-fashioned salting-down method, there is supreme pleasure awaiting you both in the preparing and in the using of the herbs.

Old-fashioned Recipe for Herb Butter   TIME: Variable

2 tbs. freshly minced herb   1 tsp. coarse butchers' salt
½ lb. salted butter   Cold tallow or paraffin

Gather herb in the early morning of a sunny day before the warmth of the air has dried all the dew.

Cut only the tenderest tops; wash if necessary under cold running water; remove leaves from stems; with a sharp knife mince leaves fine.

Place in mixing bowl; blend thoroughly with softened butter.

Pack tightly into small glass jar; cover top with thin layer coarse salt; cover with cold tallow or paraffin; seal tightly; place in *deep freeze* until needed.

When ready to use, remove fat and salt covering.

Use herb butter to flavor roast meats and sauces; but omit using additional salt until after tasting.

See also "Herb Butters" in *The Art of Cooking with Herbs and Spices* by author.

Basic Recipe for Salted-down Herbs   TIME: Variable

Selected fresh herbs   Coarse butchers' salt

Gather herbs in the early morning of a sunny day before the warmth of the air has dried all the dew.

Cut only the tenderest tops; wash if necessary under cold running water; dry on absorbent paper; strip herb leaves from the stems, except when salting *whole sprigs* of *dill* or *parsley*.

With sharp knife mince leaves fine; arrange 1-inch layer of leaves in small glass jar; sprinkle layer lightly with coarse salt; repeat until jar is filled. Top layer should be salt.

Seal jar tightly; label; place in *deep freeze* or freezing compartment of refrigerator. Will keep at least a year.

Salted herbs may be used as fresh herbs in recipes without adding salt.

Especially good in *salads, sauces, soups,* and *stews;* also over *chops, fish, poultry,* and *roast meats.*

This recipe may be prepared in any amounts, singly or in combinations as desired.

See also "Herb Blends and Bouquets" in *The Art of Cooking with Herbs and Spices* by author.

CHAPTER SEVEN

Fragrant Culinary Herb Leaves and Seed

ANGELICA or **GARDEN ANGELICA,** *Angelica archangelica officinalis,* isn't mentioned in history until during medieval times. Then many of the herbs were given names associated with phases of religion and with biblical history.

Angelica was often referred to as "the herb of the angels" and "the herb of the Holy Ghost." An infusion of angelica leaves is said to have protected the population of entire villages from the frightful scourge of the plague. And no doubt angelica derived these biblical or religious names from the superstitions which surrounded its early uses. The people really believed that the angels and the Holy Ghost had imbued the herb with its healing qualities.

Early in the seventeenth century the leaves and stems were quite commonly used to season many foods. The seed were crushed and infused in wines as flavoring; and liqueurs were given a special taste and aroma when prepared with angelica seed. Even today various liqueurs are flavored with crushed angelica seed. The stalks and stems of the herb are candied and eaten as confections or used to decorate fancy cakes and pastries.

Though the herb was not familiar to the ancient civilizations, from medieval times on it has been widely cultivated in France and Germany. Today we receive most of our seed from

57

these two countries. Seedlings may be purchased from herb garden and nurseries. The native species is commonly called **AMERICAN ANGELICA,** *Angelica atropurpurea.*

Characteristics: Angelica is a handsome, sturdy biennial which grows from 6 to 8 feet tall. This hardy herb has beautiful, large foliage shaped somewhat like the leaves of the tropical tuberous begonia. The hollow stems are 2 to 3 inches in diameter, and the blossoms are cymes of tiny white flowers. Angelica will grow in any moderately cool climate in the shade or partial shade. It may be grown also as a perennial if the flower heads are cut off as soon as they blossom. This stately herb makes a glamorous back border for the garden.

The root or rhizome has a pungent aromatic taste and has a commercial value as a medicinal ingredient as well as in confections. The oil extracted from the seed gives a sweetish flavor to custards and bread.

Uses: The entire angelica herb is useful. The tender young leaves add an intriguing new appeal to many kinds of *fish* and *shellfish* when the leaves are placed in the water in which the sea food is poached. The stalk, when blanched, may be eaten like celery or cooked as a vegetable, or prepared with sugar and eaten as we eat rhubarb. The stems and the roots are flavorings in *liqueurs* and *cordials* such as Chartreuse, Benedictine, anisette, and sometimes in gin and absinthe.

Cultivating: The seed germinate very slowly but will thrive in a deep, rich loam which is kept moist and well drained. Unless one is absolutely certain that the seed are not more than a year old, it is best to buy the plants. However, if started from fresh seed, plant in a moist seedbed in the early spring. Transplant the seedlings to a permanent location the following spring. The plants should be at least 18 inches apart in rows spaced about 3 feet. Two or three plants are sufficient for the average family use. Keep plants free from weeds by frequent cultivation.

Harvesting: Leaves. Pick the fresh, green, tender leaves and stems as needed. If stems are to be eaten as celery, then blanch the plant as for celery.

Seed. If seed are desired for candies and cookies, allow the flower umbels to mature and go to seed, but be sure to pick them just before they are completely dried in order to prevent them from shattering. Spread on a tray or clean cloth to dry in a warm, airy place, either indoors or out. Rub out the seed between the palms of the hands. Store in tightly closed opaque containers ready for use.

ANISE, *Pimpinella anisum,* with its lacy leaves and fragrant, flowering umbels, is among the oldest and most precious herbs we know. As far back as 1500 B.C. anise was listed among the medicinal herbs of the Egyptians. Centuries later Pliny (Caius Plinius Secundus, 23–79) wrote glowingly of the flavor of the anise leaves and the seed as seasonings for food. Charlemagne grew this aromatic plant in his gardens. Like so many of the ancient herbs used by the Romans, anise found its way to England. There, during medieval times, it was one of the imported herbs which were highly taxed to increase England's revenue. Undoubtedly it was the seed of the anise which provided the extra income. (Though the Bible mentions anise as a tithe, it is thought that this tiny seed was confused with the dill seed.) From England anise was brought to America by our first colonists, and from that time to this it has remained a favorite among herbs.

Characteristics: Annual, 2 feet tall, sprawls and grows slowly; lacy, deeply notched foliage, heavy cymes of yellowish-white flowers. Will grow in all temperate and hot climates. Anise is widely cultivated commercially in the very warm countries of Europe, especially in Spain, Italy, southern France, southern Russia, and Bulgaria. India, Mexico, and South America export anise seed, but the greater part of America's supply comes from the island of Jamaica.

The tiny oval seed of the anise herb grown in our gardens resembles the caraway seed in size, but there the resemblance ceases. Anise seed is greenish-gray in color and the ends are blunt rather than pointed like the caraway; and even when the seed appears brown in color, it can never be mistaken for a caraway seed, for its aroma and taste are unmistakably sweet.

The anise cultivated in the Orient is an entirely different species which belongs to the magnolia family. This anise seed, the dried fruit of an evergreen tree, the *Illicium verum,* is called STAR ANISE, BADIAN ANISE, or CHINESE ANISE. The small yellow and white flowers of the evergreen conceal the lovely star-shaped seed in dark brown beaks.

Uses: The fragrant, fresh, sweet leaves of anise add a delicate, appetizing flavor to foods such as *mixed fruit salads, cream sauces, vegetable soups,* and *stews. Shellfish,* steamed or poached in water to which several anise leaves have been added, will absorb some of the refreshing flavor of the herb.

The flowers, when powdered, are used to flavor some brands of *muscatel* and *vermouth*.

The anise seed are effectively utilized industrially, especially in perfumes, medicines, and soaps. Many *liqueurs,* and *anisette* in particular, owe their distinctive flavor to the use of the crushed seed.

Both the whole seed and the ground anise add a pleasing flavor to many foods such as *appetizers* and *canapés, cakes* and *cookies, cheese* and *fruits, meats* and *sausages,* and *fruit pies.*

Cultivating: Fresh seed should be planted in the early spring in a smooth, fairly rich, well-drained soil in a warm, sunny section of the garden. The rows should be from 2 to 3 feet apart and the seed planted at the rate of 12 to the foot and covered but ½ inch. The seedlings should be thinned to only 3 or 4 plants to the foot. A row of anise plants 6 to 8 feet long will be enough to supply the average family with both leaves and seed. Be sure to keep the ground surrounding the plants well cultivated throughout the entire growing season.

Harvesting: Leaves. The plant matures and blossoms in about 10 weeks. From then on the fresh, young leaves may be picked during the summer months as needed.

Seed: The fruiting umbels begin to turn a grayish-green early in the fall. Clip umbels from the plants and place them on a clean white cloth stretched over a screen. Place in a warm, shady spot to dry; or if more convenient, the screen may be brought indoors. When umbels are thoroughly dried, the seed can be easily separated by rubbing between the palms. Pick out all stems and wash seed carefully in cold water. Dry completely again and store in tightly covered bottles in a cool, dark place.

BALM or **LEMON BALM,** *Melissa officinalis.* Perhaps no herb has been mentioned by poets, writers, and historians as often as balm. Jeremiah in the Old Testament refers to it. Shakespeare, Poe, Charlotte Brontë, Phoebe Taylor, and countless others through the centuries have recorded the healing qualities of balm. An old Arab proverb tells us that the tea of balm leaves "makes the heart merry and joyful." And who of us at some time or another has not sighed, *"Numquid resina (balsamum) non est Galaad* [Is there no balm in Gilead]?"

The balm of Gilead referred to in this quotation is really a tree which belongs to the poplar family and is not the balm of our modern herb gardens. But the crushed leaves of this garden balm, *Melissa officinalis,* were undoubtedly the ones which the Greeks and the Orientals used in their tea and wine drinks as a soothing remedy for nerves and fever.

Characteristics: Perennial, 1½ to 2 feet tall, lies close to the ground; clusters of pale yellow flowers. Will grow in all temperate climates. Attractive to bees, balm makes a lovely border as it reaches up from 18 to 20 inches. Fragrant leaves are charming in old-fashioned bouquets.

Uses: The strongly aromatic leaves of balm are used industrially in *perfumes* and *toilet waters;* also as flavoring in *liqueurs,* especially Chartreuse and Benedictine. As a delicate culinary seasoning, the leaves and tender sprigs of balm add their flavor to many foods as well as beverages, such as *lemonades* and *wine cups* and freshly brewed *herb teas. Meats, salads, sauces, soups,* and *stuffings* may all be alluringly seasoned by the skillful use of this herb.

Cultivating: The seed are extremely small, so it is best to mix them with sand for better distribution. Balm thrives best in sandy soil, in part shade or a warm, protected spot. To secure maximum results, the seed should be sown in a window box or cold frame and the plants transplanted when about 2 or 3 inches high. The herb has a tendency to spread and lie rather close to the ground, and for this reason plants should be placed about 18 inches apart. Two or three plants will produce enough leaves for seasoning. Keep free from weeds by frequent cultivation. To increase the growth of the foliage, pinch back the first top leaves.

Harvesting: During the first season several inches of the top growth may be cut for use as soon as the herb blooms. The second season, the stems should be cut back two or three times during the season. To prepare balm for drying, the fresh-cut tops should be spread on a screen in a dark, dry room with plenty of air circulating. As soon as dried, the stems can be removed easily and the leaves placed in tightly closed containers. Store in dark room so herb retains as much color as possible.

BASIL or **SWEET BASIL,** *Ocimum basilicum,* is one of the symbols of love in Italy. This sweetly fragrant herb is given to the beloved one as a token of fidelity, and many an Italian lover can be seen with a sprig of *basilico* (basil) tucked behind his ear as he goes to meet his sweetheart. She in turn whispers the common name for basil in the Italian dialect: *"Baccia, Nicola* [Kiss me, Nicholas]."

After Keats had read Boccaccio's tender and tragic love story of Lisabetta (whose daily tears watered the pot of basil in which she had buried the head of her lover), he was inspired to write his delicate version of *Isabella,* or *The Pot of Basil.*

In India the basil plant is still revered as sacred. The Hindus for thousands of years have used basil as a symbol of reverence for their dead. Even today the ground surrounding the holy city of Pandharpur is planted only with *Ocimum basilicum sanctum,* or "holy basil." And although the Hindus no longer bury their dead, the pot of basil is still grown in memory of a beloved departed one.

Like so many of the ancient herbs of history, sweet basil found its way from the Near East, Greece, and Italy into Spain, Portugal, and England. As early as 1610 in North America the herb was cultivated in Newfoundland. Later sweet basil became a great favorite among the culinary herbs of our first colonists.

Characteristics: Annual, very hardy. All varieties of sweet basil will grow in practically all climates. Attractive to bees. Tall varieties of sweet basil grow from 2 to 2½ feet high and spread their branches equally far. The large, almost heart-shaped leaves about an inch long are light green, dark green, purple, or variegated, depending upon the exact species. White, tubular flowers grow in spikes at the top of the weedy-looking branches of the tall varieties.

The DWARF BASIL, *Ocimum minimum,* grows in both a green-leaf and a purple-leaf variety. When the tops of the herb are carefully pinched off as the young plants are growing, they will develop into beautiful little compact bushes and are attractive when used as a border plant. Some plants may be only 6 or 8 inches high, while other dwarf varieties will grow to be a foot tall. The leaves are more yellowish-green than those of the taller species, but the small white flowers are like those of the other varieties.

The ITALIAN or CURLY BASIL, *Ocimum crispum,* with its light green leaves, flourishes in window pots as well as in the garden.

The LEMON BASIL, *Ocimum citriodora,* is a more tender plant than the other varieties. Its ovate-oblong leaves are not so shiny as those of the sweet basil, *Ocimum basilicum,* but the lemon basil usually grows 18 inches tall.

Uses: All of these varieties of sweet basil are equally delicious when used as culinary seasonings. The clovelike aroma and flavor of both the fresh and the dried leaves impart a most unusual and delectable flavor to many foods such as *eggs, fat fish, game, meats, poultry, salads, shellfish, soups, stews,* and *sauces.* Sweet *vegetables* such as the *eggplant* and the first *green peas* of the season take on a matchless flavor when prepared with fresh sweet basil. In the Italian, Portuguese, and Spanish households a tomato sauce is rarely cooked without the use of sweet basil. Various *vinegars* flavored with basil are considered epicurean and impart an exotic flavor to many variations of the famous French dressing.

Cultivating: All varieties of sweet basil are easy to grow in practically all climates. The seed may be planted in early spring after all danger of frost is past. The ground should be dry, well drained, and in a sunny spot. A single row of 2 or 3 feet will be ample for the average family use. Plant 12 to 15 seed to the foot and cover to a depth of only ½ inch.

The plants of the tall, sweet basils should be spaced about 12 inches; those of the dwarf varieties at least 6 inches apart; and the Italian or curly basil needs at least 15 inches between plants. After germination, which takes from 5 to 7 days, the herb grows very quickly.

Harvesting: Flowering Tips and Leaves. The fresh, tender leaves may be used for flavoring as soon as they are large enough to pick. To provide dried basil, the herb should be cut 6 to 8 inches above the ground when the plants first begin to flower. Several cuttings of the leaves may be made during the season. Spread the cuttings very thinly on a clean dry screen placed in a shady spot. Dry the basil thoroughly, then strip the leaves and flowering tips from the stems. Pack in tightly covered opaque containers. The dried herb will have a slightly brownish-green tint. See also Chapter Six, "Quick-Freezing and Preserving Fresh Herbs."

BAY LEAF or **LAUREL LEAF,** *Laurus nobilis,* is the aromatic leaf of the small, evergreen sweet-bay or laurel tree. Though bay leaves are among the oldest of European herbs, this evergreen now is cultivated extensively in Central America and our Southern states.

Like many of the aromatic herbs, the leaves of fragrant bay were woven into wreaths of honor for Greek and Roman heroes and kings. In Greece the green bay flourished and was called the Daphne tree in honor of the beautiful mythical nymph. It was Daphne, daughter of the river god Paneus, who, when she was pursued by Leucippus and then by Apollo, was saved by being transformed into an evergreen laurel tree.

In the time of Cicero (106–43 B.C.) wedding cakes were baked on a bed of bay leaves, and the Latin proverb: *Loreolam in mustaceo quaerere,* to look for a bay leaf in a wedding cake, became the popular one which led to another version: *Acum in meta foeni quaerere,* to look for a needle in a pyramid of hay. This finally became the universally favored phrase: "Like looking for a needle in a haystack."

Characteristics: The true laurel is an evergreen shrub or small tree native to Asia Minor and the Mediterranean countries. It is now cultivated in England, Central America, and in the Southern part of the United States, especially in North and South Carolina and Georgia. The laurel which grows in California is much larger and is known as *Umbellularia californica.* The laurel grown in America has the same beautiful green, waxy, elliptical leaves as the European laurels. They vary in size from 1 to 3 inches in length and may be from ½ to 1 inch or more at the widest part, or the middle of the leaf. The undersides are a pale yellowish-green, and the leaves taper to points at the base and the tip. The laurel tree of Greece is the tallest of these trees, often reaching a height of 60 feet, and its foliage is almost tropically luxuriant.

Uses: The essential oil of the bay or laurel leaf is an ingredient in some perfumes, but the chief use of this exceedingly aromatic leaf is as a culinary herb seasoning. Its naturally bitter taste is transformed into a delicious and tempting seasoning when used with many foods such as *fish, game, meats, pickles, poultry, salads, sauces, soups, stews, stuffings,* and *vegetables.*

Cultivating: The *Laurus nobilis* needs special care when grown farther north than Georgia. It is not a hardy plant for the out-of-doors, but it adds a great deal of charm to an herb garden and will grow well as a tub plant if great care is given it.

The potting mixture must be prepared with real skill and

should consist of 2 parts loam, 2 parts sand, 2 parts peat moss and fertilizer, preferably cow manure.

The tubbed laurel may be placed in the garden in April in a sunny spot and the soil should be kept moist at all times. In October, or when frost threatens, the plant should be placed in a protecting shed or a shaded greenhouse where the temperature never falls below 38° F. nor goes above 45° F. The plant cannot stand the dry heat of a room and will die if taken into the house.

Harvesting: Like most herbs, bay leaves should be picked in the early morning when they are clean and still fresh from the morning dew but not wet. Place leaves on a clean white cloth stretched over a screen and allow to dry gradually in a warm, shady spot. When dry but not brittle, arrange each leaf on a clean, hard tray over which a white cloth has been carefully stretched. Cover dried leaves with another clean cloth and place a smooth lightweight board over them. Press the leaves flat by weighing the board down with an object weighing not more than a pound. Allow the weight to stay over the leaves for at least 10 days. This prevents the leaves from curling up, and at best they are somewhat undulant. When completely dried and pressed, pack carefully in tightly covered opaque containers until needed.

BERGAMOT or **WILD BERGAMOT,** *Monarda fistulosa,* is found in the fields and meadows of our Western states, and from British Columbia across the continent to Quebec, and as far south as North Carolina.

Our early colonists learned the use of the bergamots from the American Indians, and to this day the RED BERGAMOT, *Monarda didyma,* is still called Oswego tea, the common name given to the herb because it was used by the Oswego tribe in preparing an herb tea. This tribe and numerous others are still fond of Oswego tea and drink it regularly in place of the oriental teas. At one time in early colonial history, when there was a boycott on British imports, Oswego tea was the only tea the colonists would drink.

Our native wild bergamot was taken to France in the early eighteenth century, and it became one of the most useful of cultivated herbs. France uses the oil of bergamot in the preparation of her most expensive and exotic perfumes.

The bergamot found in Europe is a tree of the citrus family which is cultivated extensively in the city of Bergamo, Italy. The oil of the tree's tiny orange-flavored fruit is used commercially only and chiefly in perfumes. This bergamot is in no way related to our native herb.

Characteristics: A handsome, hardy perennial, 2 or 3 feet tall, with beautiful, fragrant, cottony foliage and clusters of mauve flowers. May be cultivated and will grow in practically all temperate and cool climates. Attractive as a clumpy back-border plant. Lovely in any garden, beautiful in bouquets, and attractive to bees.

Other popular species of this native North American herb are the LEMON BERGAMOT, *Monarda citriodora,* with its lemony aroma, and the red bergamot, with brilliant crimson corollas. The latter is also commonly called Oswego tea, FRA-GRANT BALM, INDIAN'S PLUME, BEE BALM, or RED BALM. All these *Monardas* are easily propagated and are among the most beautiful of tall herbs. They blossom during July and August and add brilliant color to midsummer gardens and attract bees.

Uses: The volatile oil of the red and the wild bergamots, like the other members of the mint, *Labiatae,* family, are of industrial value in the preparation of perfumes and pomades. The oil adds a pleasing scent to them and to certain chemicals such as naphthalene and iodoform. The most popular culinary use of the dried leaves is as an *herb tea.* The fresh leaves and small sprigs of bergamot are a colorful *garnish* for *fruit* and *wine drinks,* as well as a subtle addition to the flavor.

Cultivating: Propagation is by seed or root division. Seed may be sown in a cold frame during late July or August and transplanted in the spring. Or the seed may be sown in the outdoor seedbed in November. It will germinate the following spring and reach its complete growth during the second year. All transplanting and root division should take place in the early spring.

Bergamot thrives best in a moist soil and the shade. The plants spread quickly and should be allowed at least 18 inches for growing. The fibrous roots should be dug up every three years and only the newer outside roots replanted. The center should be thrown away.

Harvesting: If large blossoms are desired, the herb should not be allowed to blossom the first year. The second year, it may be cut back after the first blooming and will bloom a second time during the autumn. Cut all stalks and mulch (cover) with rich soil during the winter.

For culinary uses, cut the tender young stems just before the plant blossoms and on a hot day after the dew has evaporated. Dry on a small screen or tray covered with cheesecloth and placed in a warm, shady spot. Strip the leaves carefully from stems and store in tightly covered containers.

BORAGE, *Borago officinalis,* has been among those herbs most universally favored since the time of the ancient Greeks.

Its leafy tips, placed in a cooling drink, are said to bring a pleasant forgetfulness of all troublesome thoughts. Pliny recorded that the delicious flavor of borage would drive away all sorrows and bring courage to those who crushed and blended the aromatic, cooling leaves and flowering tips of borage in a cup of ruby wine. The English, too, have always associated borage with courage. In fact, they pronounce the name of the herb as though it rhymed with courage.

By the early fifteenth century the cucumberlike flavor of borage was used to season wild game and hare. The English also combined the fresh green herb with other greens of the vegetable garden and served the mixture as a vegetable. The western Europeans liked borage as a cooked vegetable and often ate the tenderest leaves raw in salads.

This beautiful herb with its thick clusters of star-shaped heavenly-blue blossoms is one of the most profuse wild flowers of Sicily. Its wild beauty and loveliness are found also all along the coast of the blue Mediterranean.

Characteristics: Borage is a sturdy, luxuriant annual which grows from 2 to 2½ feet tall. The foliage is coarse and covered with grayish hairs which give it a fuzzy appearance, and the large, almost pinnate leaves look grayish-green because of their hairy surface. The exquisite star-shaped blue flowers with long tapering stamens blossom singly at the tip of the stalk. The young leaves lose their mild cooling flavor after the herb has blossomed. The roots of the plant are delicate, and seedlings always should be snipped off close to the ground or thinned out instead of being transplanted. Borage will grow in all temperate and warm climates. Bees are attracted to the beautiful flowers. It is a lovely plant for hilly grounds and sloping rock gardens.

Uses: The young leaves and flowering tips are used to flavor *iced drinks, salads, herb teas,* and *vegetables.* The exquisite *flowers* may be *crystallized* in the manner of rose petals and violets. The Europeans cook the tender leaves and eat them as we eat spinach and other green leafy vegetables.

Both the dried and the fresh leaves are used to flavor *soups* and *stews* and may take the place of parsley in these preparations.

Cultivating: Like so many of the herbs, borage will grow in a light, poor, dry soil where there is plenty of sun. The seed germinate quickly and the plant grows best if not transplanted. It also resows itself freely. Seed may be sown in rows a foot apart and the seedlings thinned to allow a space of from 10 to 12 inches for each mature plant. A dozen plants will supply the average family. If a continuous supply of the tenderest young leaves is desired, the second planting should take place 6 weeks after the first.

Plant borage at the top of a hill or on sloping ground so the full beauty of the drooping blossoms may be seen.

Harvesting: Pick the fresh tender leaves for greens before the plant blossoms. Snip off carefully as in picking spinach. The young flowering tips may be cut as soon as the first blue petals appear. For use in soups and potpourris, the leaves, flowering tips, and stems may be cut as other herbs. Then dry on clean white cheesecloth or screen placed in dry, shady spot. When thoroughly dried, flowers and leaves may be picked from stems and stored separately in tightly covered opaque containers.

BURNET or **SALAD BURNET,** *Sanguisorba minor,* was used chiefly for its astringent, medicinal qualities during ancient and medieval times.

The fresh foliage was crushed and placed on the wounds of soldiers while on the field of battle. The ancient Chinese made a plaster of the dried burnet leaves and applied it as a styptic to stop profuse bleeding.

The GREAT BURNET, *Sanguisorba officinalis,* grows wild in the meadows of Europe and Asia. During the Middle Ages its tender young leaves were eaten as a salad. Wine drinks were garnished and flavored with the crushed leaves.

The wild burnet which is found in the Eastern states and is now widely cultivated in the Southern states isn't the same species as that which grows wild in Europe and Asia. We have no great burnet anywhere in America. However, the two species of burnet which our colonists brought to America in 1672 were undoubtedly the burnets which belong to the rose family. Another burnet, called *Pimpinella saxifraga L.*, and well known to the ancient Greeks and still found in profusion throughout all of Central Europe, is entirely unknown to America.

Characteristics: A perennial, almost evergreen, 1 to 2 feet tall; luxuriant feathery foliage forms neat clumps close to the earth. Rose-colored and white flowers form flat umbels. Burnet makes a lovely border plant. Will grow in all temperate and warm climates.

Uses: Young leaves used as flavoring in *salads* and *beverages*. Dried leaves as flavoring for *vinegars;* also as an *herb tea*.

Cultivating: The plants germinate from seed sown very early in the spring. A dry, poor, sandy soil in a sunny spot is best, and the plant grows more luxurious if not transplanted. Therefore, the weak seedlings should be pinched off to allow the spacing of from 10 to 15 inches for the root clumps to mature. The plant may also be propagated by root division.

Harvesting: The small, tender young leaves may be used constantly and the plant kept blooming all summer if the herb is cut back when it is not more than 5 inches high. The almost evergreen clumps of foliage will thrive all winter in most climates.

CAMOMILE, GERMAN or **HUNGARIAN,** *Matricaria chamomilla,* has been noted for its healing qualities and has been used for such from the time of the early Egyptians down to our modern day. The tea brewed from the dried camomile blossoms can reduce fever and inflammation in wounds and slight sprains. I remember many a time a tiny wounded finger was healed of its cuts and bruises by being bathed in the soothing warmth of a camomile tea prepared by my loving mother. And once in Switzerland a foot injured in mountain climbing was saved from a serious infection by hourly applications of strong camomile tea while waiting for the doctor to arrive.

Characteristics: German or Hungarian camomile is a hardy annual, 15 inches high, with delicate lacy foliage and white daisy-shaped flowers which distinguish all the varieties of camomile. Most attractive to bees, it resembles the ROMAN or ENGLISH CAMOMILE, *Anthemis nobilis,* and blossoms about 2 months after planting. German camomile will grow in all temperate and warm climates.

Roman or English camomile is also hardy. It is a low, creeping perennial and makes a lovely border or ground covering. It, too, will thrive in practically all the temperate and warm climates.

Uses: Dried flower heads of the Roman or English camomile are used chiefly in preparing *herb teas*. In many European countries even today, camomile tea is used in place of regular tea and coffee. The oil of the camomiles adds fragrance to perfumes, cosmetics, and blends of tobaccos.

Cultivating: The German or Hungarian camomile may be sown in the early spring or the late summer, since the plants will bloom in about 8 weeks. Also the seed sown early in the fall will produce plants that will blossom early the following spring. The seed may be sown in drills and barely covered with soil, or they may be broadcast, since the plant spreads rapidly and will crowd out all weeds.

The Roman or English camomile is much more satisfactory as an ornamental herb, for it will blossom from the middle of summer until killed by the frost. This species will grow in any good, dry soil in a sunny spot. Early in the spring seed may be sown or the herb may be propagated by root divisions. If planted in rows, the root divisions should be set about 9 inches apart and only lightly covered with soil. At first a little hand weeding should be done, but as the runners spread, weeding is no longer necessary, for the weeds will have no place in which to grow.

Harvesting: When the plants are in full bloom, the flower heads should be gathered and spread thinly on canvas sheets and dried quickly in the sun. All leaves and stems should then be removed, and when the flowers are completely dry they should be put in tightly covered containers and stored in a cool, dry place.

CARAWAY, *Carum carvi,* was made known to the ancient Egyptians by the traders who brought caraway into Egypt with them from Arabia. And the tiny, pungent seed are still as popular and as widely used as they were those many centuries ago.

Claudius Galen (130–200?), the Greek physician and medical writer, mentions the goodness of caraway and its beneficial properties. The ancient Swiss and Romans cultivated the herb, and Charlemagne (742–814) grew caraway in his gardens.

Though we know caraway chiefly for its seed, both the French and the English used its feathery leaves in soups and salads as early as the fifteenth century. By the sixteenth century they had discovered that the caraway root when boiled had a most delicious flavor. Even today in Switzerland and Germany the slender caraway root is often eaten as a vegetable.

Characteristics: A hardy biennial, sometimes called a perennial since it self-sows year after year. Caraway has beautiful feathery leaves and grows about 2 feet tall. Its creamy or yellowish-white flowers grow in umbels at the tips of slender stems. Caraway will grow in any temperate or northern climate.

The root, about 8 inches long, is slender and a light yellow in color which turns almost oyster-white when it is cooked.

The caraway seed are less than ¼ inch long and are dark brown with pale yellow edges. The seed curve to resemble the delicate crescent moon.

Uses: The fresh leaves impart delicious flavor to foods such as *cheeses, meats, salads, soups,* and *vegetables.* The roots may be steamed and eaten as a vegetable. The seed are used as seasoning in *soups, meats, vegetables, breads, cakes,* and *pastries,* and are often sugar-coated and eaten as a confection. The distinctive and delicious flavor of the oil extracted from the seed is the base of one of the most popular liqueurs, called kümmel. Other industrial uses are made of the essential caraway oil, especially in soaps and perfumes.

Cultivating: The seed may be sown in the spring or autumn. If sown in the springtime, the herb will grow from 6 to 8 inches tall the first season, and the green, feathered foliage will form a cluster resembling carrot leaves. If the seed are sown in the autumn, the herb will be ready to harvest for seed during the early summer. The plant will also self-sow year after year. A single row but a few feet long will produce enough seed for the average family's use.

Since germination is slow and the root is long and delicate, caraway should be planted where it can be left undisturbed. It lends itself as a beautiful background for other herbs in the garden. The seed should be planted in a dry, light, well-drained soil in rows 2 feet apart and covered to a depth of about ½ inch. Twelve seed to the foot will produce about 6 plants. Cultivate well and keep free from weeds since the plants grow slowly at first and need this care.

Harvesting: Leaves. The fresh, young leaves may be picked as soon as the herb is well established. If not grown to produce seed, the flowering stems are attractive in bouquets.

Seed. The caraway seed may be harvested during the second season. When the fruiting umbels have turned brown they should be cut from the plant before they dry and shatter. The umbels may be dried on a white cloth placed on a tray or screen either in the sun or the shade. When thoroughly dried, the seed are easily separated by rubbing between tne palms of the hands. Clean out all stems, and store seed in tightly closed opaque containers. Use as desired.

CARDAMOM SEED, *Elleteria cardamomum maton,* though not a garden herb in our hemisphere, is mentioned here because it is one of the culinary herb seed included in the companion volume: *The Art of Cooking with Herbs and Spices.*

The cardamom plant, with its thick woody roots, belongs to the *Zingiberaceae* family. The tall plant, native to India, grows there from 8 to 12 feet high and is cultivated on a large commercial scale. At present cardamom plants are being cultivated to some extent in both Central America and Mexico.

The cardamom seed is the seed of the dried fruit of the cardamom plant. There are from 8 to 16 irregularly and oval-shaped seed in each pod or unopened fruit capsule. The capsule averages about ½ inch long and ¼ inch thick and is covered with a paperlike but tough fiber of greenish-brown. Some of the unopened dried pods are marketed unbleached; others are bleached to a creamy white. The aroma of the unopened capsule is only slightly aromatic and unusually pleasant to the taste.

The cardamom seed grow within the pods or capsules in groups of from 8 to 16. They are irregular and somewhat angular in shape and not more than ³⁄₃₂ of an inch long and less than ¹⁄₁₆ of an inch thick.

The cardamom plant, a luxuriant perennial, requires more than 3 years' growth before it bears fruit. After the third year the crops are regular and abundant. When the fruit matures and after it is harvested, the entire plant is dug up and transplanted.

In the process of transplanting, the old stem dies and a new plant begins its growth. The second year after the transplanting, the new cardamom plant bears its fruit, and so the process is continued from year to year. While one group of plants is developing, another group bears fruit.

Like the majority of tropical herbs and spices, the cardamoms, as the fruit are called, are dried in the sun. They are graded according to the size of the capsules, and the whole ones are packed in cases weighing more than a hundred pounds, ready for shipment to the spice traders.

Uses: The minute, whole cardamom seed are used in some of the superior whole pickling spice blends. The ground seed are used in blends of curry powder, also in combination with other prepared spice seasonings such as for sausages and prepared meats.

The Arabs and the East Indians used cardamom earlier than 800 B.C., and even today they chew the seed as a candy. Ground cardamom is a favorite seasoning in many Mexican and Spanish dishes.

The whole seed, as well as the ground cardamom, are great favorites with the Scandinavians, who use them extensively as a flavoring in sweet *pastries* and *cookies.* This exotic herb seed, either whole or ground, adds a most intriguing flavor to many of the old favorites such as *bread, rolls, cookies, fruit salads, gelatins, jellies,* and hot, spiced *wine drinks.*

CATNIP or **CATMINT,** *Nepeta cataria,* was used only as a culinary herb early in the fifteenth century. Meats were rubbed with the fresh leaves, and the herb was considered a wonderfully healthful addition to the traditional early-spring mixed green salad.

Medieval history tells us that the botanical name, *Nepeta cataria,* was given to the herb by the Tuscans, who found it growing wild in great profusion in their village called Nept. And we read that the early Romans, French, English, and Germans drank catnip tea for many centuries before the Orientals introduced the teas of the Far East. Even today catnip tea is a great favorite with many Europeans.

Early American history tells us that Captain John Mason was the first person to bring catnip to America and plant it in an herb garden in Newfoundland. The coastal fishermen used the leaves to brew themselves a strong tonic. Legend says that a tea made from the foliage of catnip gives courage to the timid and makes the weak strong.

Soon after our early settlers planted catnip in Salem they taught the American Indians how to brew and drink a strong catnip tea. The Indians took to this native drink with genuine enthusiasm and claimed that a brew of catnip tea induced a sound and restful sleep. To this day the tea has remained a favorite drink with many of our surviving tribes.

Characteristics: Catnip is a tall, hardy perennial with attractive heart-shaped, gray-green, fragrant foliage with dense spikes of blue or mauve blossoms. It is attractive to bees in the herb garden. Will grow in practically all temperate climates of the world.

Uses: Leaves used principally in preparing herb teas and as a tidbit for "pussy." The oil has a limited medicinal value in some sedatives.

Cultivating: Catnip does well in almost any type of soil but thrives more luxuriantly when planted in well-drained, fairly rich loam. If a more fragrant herb is desired, it should be grown in sandy soil. Catnip may be propagated either by seed or division. The seed may be sown in early spring or late in the fall. Fall-sown seed gives a heavier growth. When the plants have reached a height of 4 inches they should be thinned to stand in rows from 12 to 16 inches apart. A small amount of shallow cultivation will favor a vigorous growth.

Harvesting: The flowering tops and leaves are harvested when the plants are in full bloom. Cut them and place on screens or small trays in a warm but shady spot. When thoroughly dried, pack in tightly covered containers and store in a cool, dark place so the leaves will retain their natural green color.

CELERY, *Apium graveolens,* as we know it today, was developed from a wild, bitter herb found growing in the salt marshes of Europe and Asia. For centuries the Chinese used wild celery, sometimes called SMALLAGE, solely for medicinal purposes, and the Abyssinians thought it good only for stuffing pillows.

It wasn't until the ancient Greeks and Romans introduced blanching the bunches of wild celery that it was used as flavoring in meats and salads. When the wild herb was hilled up with warm, damp earth, the strong, bitter taste was lessened. Charlemagne cultivated the *Apium* and ordered his subjects to plant the herb in their gardens, for during all its early history celery was regarded as a luxury herb. As its flavor grew milder and sweeter through improved cultivation, the Italians bravely began using the herb as a separate food. They ate the celery stalks raw and boiled the roots as a vegetable.

It was not until early in the nineteenth century that celery began to be widely cultivated in America. By about 1880 celery growing had become an industry, and today this once humble weed of southern Europe holds sixth place among the fresh vegetables produced for our markets.

Characteristics: Plant. A hardy biennial, sometimes an annual; pale green pinnate foliage; tiny white flower heads which grow in large umbels at tips of slender stems. Will grow in all temperate climates but requires specific growing conditions in specific localities. In the states along the Atlantic Coast, two popular varieties are grown commercially: a bleached, white celery called GOLDEN HEART, and a slower-growing large, green-stalked variety called PASCAL. California supplies our markets with tons of Pascal celery, and in the central part of California vast celery farms cultivate the celery for its seed.

Seed. Celery seed are tiny mericarps less than $\frac{1}{16}$ of an inch long, and the natural bitterness of these infinitesimal light brown dried fruits adds marvelous flavor to many foods.

Uses: The entire herb is used chiefly as a culinary flavoring: the leaves, the seed, and the stalks. The complete stalk is one of our standard vegetables both raw and cooked.

Cultivating: Plant. It isn't easy to grow celery, and gardeners have been developing varieties which will thrive in specific and particular localities. Most books on vegetable gardening will give detailed information on the culture of celery, and most seed catalogues contain explicit directions on its care.

It is much safer and easier for the amateur to buy the celery plants. However, if you are adventuresome, one small package of seed will provide more celery than the average family can use in a season. Sow the seed in an outdoor seedbed or cold frame. In about 2 months the tiny plants will be ready for transplanting. Celery requires rich, moist soil and a great deal of care. After another 2 months, when the celery is about half grown, the blanching process may begin.

Commercial blanching methods: Commercial fields of celery are usually blanched with boards or a special heavy, water-proof celery-blanching paper, though many of the commercial growers near our large Eastern cities still blanch the giant Pascal celery with soil.

When boards are used for blanching, they are hauled to the field and placed alongside the rows of celery. The boards are held in place by wire spanners which straddle the celery rows and hold the two boards for each row in place.

If the celery is blanched with paper, the heavy rolls are set on end alongside the celery, and as the paper is unrolled it is held in place by wire spanners which straddle the rows. The spanners are set at sufficient depth in the ground so they hold the heavy paper close to the celery plants. After the blanching period of from 10 days to 2 weeks, the paper is rolled up and may be used a second or third time during a season. Several different machines have been developed which roll and unroll the paper for this type of blanching.

The quickest way to blanch celery in a small garden is to hill up the soil around the plants, making sure to hold the foliage together so that the earth doesn't get into the hearts of the plants.

Seed. If the celery plants are grown chiefly for seed, they must be well mulched with straw to prevent winter-killing in sections of the country where there is severe freezing weather. The seed form on the flower stalks only after the second season.

Harvesting: Plant. In cold climates the celery literally may be transplanted, roots and all, to a cool basement. Simply pack the celery stalks closely in boxes and surround the plants with moist soil. In warm climates the celery may be left in the ground and harvested as needed.

Seed. When the fruiting umbels are mature and have turned brown they may be cut and placed on a clean white cloth stretched over a screen. Dry in a warm, shady place where there is plenty of circulating air. Separate the seed by rubbing the dried umbels between the palms. Remove all twigs. Store the clean seed in tightly closed opaque containers ready for use as desired.

CHERVIL, *Anthriscus cerefolium,* was used as a garden vegetable by the ancient Greeks and Romans. They utilized the entire herb. The foliage was cooked as we now cook spinach, and they ate the roots as we now eat other root vegetables.

In the ninth century chervil was one of the herbs grown in the famous gardens of the Benedictine monastery in St. Gall,

Switzerland; and Charlemagne included this beautifully vivid herb in his herb gardens. In Saxon England chervil was a favorite potherb, and the Saxons used the tender young leaves to flavor soups and as an ingredient in green salads.

Characteristics: A tall hardy annual from 18 inches to 2 feet in height which resembles parsley. The lacy, delicate, fern-like deep green foliage is a beautiful sight in a green garden. The tiny white flowers grow in umbels. Chervil requires a light, well-drained soil and thrives best in the shade or partial shade. Will grow in all temperate zones.

Uses: The tender young leaves, both fresh and dried, are used as culinary flavoring and also as an attractive garnish. The tuberous variety is cooked as other root vegetables and is a most unusual addition to the vegetable garden.

Cultivating: The seed should be planted early in the spring in a partially shaded, moist permanent location where the mature plants will be allowed to stand. Even though chervil does not transplant easily, it is not difficult to grow. The shallow drills should be about 2 feet apart and 12 to 15 seed allotted to each foot. As soon as the seedlings are an inch or two high they should be thinned until 4 inches apart in the row. Cultivate the same as for carrots and handle carefully until plants are well established.

Harvesting: Within 6 to 8 weeks from the time of sowing the tender young leaves may be cut and used as desired. Later in the season the leaves may be cut and dried rapidly in the shade. Small amounts may be placed on trays covered with white cheesecloth; larger amounts may be dried on screens.

Store clean, dry leaves in tightly covered containers.

CHIVES, *Allium schoenoprasum,* were known to the Chinese as early in history as 3000 B.C. Like their more pungent relative, the onion, chives were used all over Asia and northern Europe centuries before the beginning of the Christian Era. From that time to this the mild, delicate flavor of chives has remained one of the most popular of culinary seasonings. Chives' history is one with that of the ancient Egyptians and the Romans. The clumps of tubular leaves and pompons of lavender flowers have graced the herb gardens of kings and monarchs; and the delicate flavoring has been known in the kitchens of many a secluded monastery from the shores of Lake Constance in Switzerland to those of southern France and Italy.

Characteristics: Chives are a hardy perennial, 8 to 10 inches high. The slender, dark green, tubular leaves grow in clumps, and the flowers are tiny lavender-colored pompons. Chives require rich, rocky soil and plenty of sun and will grow especially well indoors or out, in all temperate and warm climates. The plant makes a charming and decorative border or edging which adds color and interest to a rock garden.

Uses: The fresh leaves are a most popular culinary seasoning in such foods as *appetizers, cheeses, butter, eggs, sauces, soups,* and *salad dressings.* The dried leaves are powdered and prepared with *sodium chloride* as an herb salt. The tiny bulbs may be pulled and pickled as one pickles small onions.

Cultivating: Chives may be grown from seed planted in a rich, pebbly soil, but germination is slow, and the usual method of propagation (as well as the easiest) is to plant a clump of 2 or 3 tiny bulbs. The bulbs multiply so quickly that it is advisable to dig them up every 2 or 3 years and subdivide the clumps to prevent overcrowding. The bulbs should be set from 6 to 10 inches apart in a sunny place and kept well cultivated and free from weeds. In the late fall one or two clumps may be potted or planted in an indoor window box. The fresh, tender shoots will continue growing for use all winter.

Harvesting: Simply cut the slender, tubular leaves as needed. After the flower stalks have blossomed, cut them off close to the ground. Dig or pull bulbs as in pulling small onions.

> *And the manna was as coriander seed, and the colour thereof as the colour of bdellium. And the people went about, and gathered it, and ground it in mills, or beat it in a mortar, and baked it in pans, and made cakes of it: and the taste of it was as the taste of fresh oil.* —NUMBERS 11:7, 8

CORIANDER SEED, *Coriandrum sativum,* is probably one of the first of the group of herbs and spices ever used in cookery. More than 5,000 years B.C. the Chinese ate the boiled root as a vegetable and flavored candies, cakes, and beverages with the seed. Moses and the Hebrews knew it well, for it is mentioned in the Old Testament more than once.

The Greeks also were familiar with coriander, for Anacreon (563?–478 B.C.) mentions it. Caesar's Roman legions brought the seed with them into northern Europe and England. The monks of St. Gall, along the shores of Lake Constance, grew the coriander in their herb gardens, and Charlemagne also cultivated it.

Characteristics: Plant. The coriander foliage is as beautiful as a lacy fern, and the lower leaves are broad and deeply lobed. The upper leaves are very narrow, and the strikingly delicate pale pink flowers blossom profusely in umbels like the other herbs of the parsley, *Umbelliferae,* family. The herb may grow as high as 2 feet, but the average height is usually a dainty 10 to 12 inches. The foliage, though extremely graceful and attractive-looking, is not fragrant.

Seed. The small, globular, yellowish-brown seed have nine ridges and are from ⅛ to ¼ inch in diameter. When dried they have a sweetish taste and an incredibly delicate aroma. The crushed or ground coriander seed have an appealing flavor which resembles a mixture of lemon peel and sage.

Uses: The whole seed are often sugar-coated and eaten as a *confection.* The crushed, powdered, or ground seed are used industrially to add flavor to *liqueurs, gin,* some *vermouths,* and as a sweet scent in *perfumes* and *toilet waters.* Their many flavoring uses in cookery are extraordinary, varying from *sausages* and *frankfurters* to *cookies* and *gingerbread.* Many Italian cooks will season *polenta* with coriander, and it is good in many other foods such as *cheese, fruits, meats, pickles, puddings, salads, soups,* and even in a *demitasse.*

Cultivating: Coriander grows easily in a wide range of conditions but thrives best in sunny locations in a well-drained soil which is medium rich. The seed germinate readily and should be planted about 1 inch deep in rows 15 to 20 inches apart, in the late spring when danger of frost is over. When the seedlings are about 3 inches high they should be thinned to 10 inches by merely pinching them off at the ground. Because of the delicate root system, *the herb is not suited to transplanting.*

Early May plantings will bloom in about 9 weeks, and the seed usually mature early in August. Keep the plant well cultivated and free from weeds at all times.

Harvesting: The seed should be harvested as soon as ripe, and to prevent excessive shattering should be cut in the early morning when the plant is wet with dew. Dry the stalks on a screen or tray placed in a warm, dry, shady place. When thoroughly dried, the seed will fall out and can be easily separated from the dried leaves. Allow the seed to dry well before storing in tightly covered containers.

CORN SALAD, *Valerianella lacustra,* is sometimes called FIELD SALAD. This name may have been given to the herb since for centuries it has grown wild in the fields of Europe and England. When its use as a salad plant was discovered, this small, retiring little weed of the fields was extensively cultivated by the early seventeenth century.

Like many of our culinary herbs which are now widely cultivated, corn salad was brought to America during the early part of the nineteenth century. It achieved immediate popularity, which it still maintains throughout most of the United States.

Characteristics: Annual, hardy, 8 to 10 inches tall. Small spoon-shaped, gray-green foliage with a mild, cool flavor something like lettuce. The pale blue flowers grow in cymes. Corn salad requires moderately rich soil, plenty of water, and will grow in all temperate climates.

Uses: Corn salad leaves are used as a *green salad* and also as a *garnish* for *cooked meats* and *sea-food salads.* The leaves, either cooked separately or in combination with other greens, make a most attractive and flavorful vegetable.

Cultivating: Corn salad is very easy to grow, and the seed may be planted in the early spring much as one plants lettuce seed. If a continuing summer supply is desired, the seed may be planted every 2 weeks for a new growth. Tiny plants should be thinned to 6 inches apart in rows spaced from 12 to 15 inches. Keep well watered during dry periods and the leaves will always have a tasty flavor and remain tender.

Harvesting: Cut the green, tender leaves as desired.

COSTMARY, *Chrysanthemum balsamita,* is popularly known as BIBLELEAF since its broad long leaves were sometimes used as bookmarks in the Bibles of the early colonists. The English common name of ALECOST was given the herb because at one time costmary was a common flavoring in beers and ales.

Like many of our best-loved herbs, costmary was known to the early Egyptians, Greeks, and Romans. Charlemagne grew the fragrant herb in his gardens; and the French, Swiss, and Spanish cooks combined costmary with other culinary herbs as early as the ninth century.

Eventually costmary found its way into the English gardens of the sixteenth century, and today the herb (brought here by the early colonists) may be found growing wild along the country roads in the Eastern and Midwestern part of the United States.

Characteristics: A large, fragrant perennial which grows in clumps from 3 to 4 feet high. The luxuriant foliage with the beautiful yellow, buttonlike blossoms makes a most attractive flower border. Costmary requires dry soil and plenty of shade. It will grow in all temperate zones.

Uses: The fresh leaves are used to flavor foods and beverages such as *cakes, game, meats, poultry,* and *herb teas.*

Cultivating: Plants may be started either from seed or from divisions of the roots. If from seed, plant them in a window box early in the spring, and transplant the young seedlings at least 2 feet apart in a bed where they may remain undisturbed for several seasons. The whole plant grows up from the roots like rhubarb, and a dry soil in the shade will give the most luxuriant foliage. If flowers are wanted, they will blossom only in the sun. Every 3 years the plants should be dug up and divided.

Harvesting: The fresh leaves may be pulled any time during the season as rhubarb is pulled, and may be used either fresh or dried. To dry, the freshly pulled leaves may be spread on a screen or clean tray in a dark, airy room. Then strip the leaves from the stalks and store in tightly covered containers for use as desired.

CRESS or **LAND CRESS,** *Lepidium sativum.* See also Water Cress.

Characteristics: Annual, 3 to 6 inches tall, hardy, tiny clusters of white blossoms. Will grow in partial shade in practically all climates, and even in a standard window box if soil is kept moist and enriched. This peppery little annual is also called PEPPERGRASS. Other species of the land cresses not as well known are the BELLE ISLE CRESS, *Barbarea verna,* and a fast-disappearing variety called ROCKET CRESS.

CUMIN SEED or **COMINO,** *Cuminum cyminum,* is another of the herb spices which historically predates the Christian Era. The ancient Persian, Greek, and Roman writings refer to both the ground cumin and the whole seed. The Romans discovered that the spiciness of the cumin might sometimes be used in the place of pepper when the latter was too expensive and difficult to secure. They developed a commercial market for cumin and sold the seed in great quantities, especially in Rome, where the masses couldn't afford the high price of pepper. When the seed were ground and the oil not extracted, the resultant oily product could be spread on bread.

By the time of Christ whole cumin seed had increased so much in value that they were considered as a tithe, just as anise seed, *aneton* or dill, and mint.

As the aromatic flavor of the infinitesimal seed grew in popularity, its uses spread from the Roman Empire and the East up through the continent of Europe and from there into Saxony. The Saxon cooks imported cumin and developed new culinary uses for both the whole and the ground seed. They learned to season poultry by sprinkling the powdered cumin over hens and peacocks before roasting them for special banquets and festive celebrations.

Like many of our present-day herbs and spices, cumin has its association with ancient superstitions and legendry. It is said that the early philosophers praised paleness as a mark of genuine scholarship. When a student appeared pale and wan while attending classes, he was considered among the favored and more brilliant of scholars. And when Pliny wrote that eating large quantities of cumin seed might cause this studious paleness, many a not-too-studious scholar would drink cumin seed oil to make him look pale, as though he had studied long into the night.

The ancient Greeks often called a miser a "bean-splitter," and when they encountered a particularly niggardly one, they would ridicule him with the taunt that he was so stingy he would even try to split a cumin seed. Today in Greece a stingy person is referred to as a "cumin-skimmer."

Characteristics: The cumin plant rarely grows more than 5 or 6 inches high because its stem is usually crooked. Even when the plant grows in its native warm climates it is never more than a foot tall. The broad, compound leaves are divided into narrow filaments. The heavy cymes of white and sometimes lavender flowers blossom at the top of the weak stems and weigh them down.

Though the herb is a delicate one which requires careful cultivation and must be kept free of weeds at all times, cumin will grow in our Northern gardens and in the Gulf Coast and

Pacific Coast states. It will thrive even in the dried regions of the West and the Southwest if properly irrigated.

There is another species of cumin native to the Mediterranean regions which is widely cultivated in India. It is the BLACK CUMIN, *Nigella sativa,* almost unknown in this country. Both the whole and the ground seed of the black cumin are used extensively in all oriental cookery.

Uses: Both the whole and the ground seed are used to season *appetizers, breads, cookies, cheeses, eggs, fish, poultry, game, fruit pies, meats,* and *vegetables.* The ground seed is often one of the ingredients in various blends of curry powder.

Commercially the seed sometimes are used to add flavor to liquors and liqueurs such as kümmel and crème de menthe. The oil is used in the compounding of medicines.

Cultivating: Seed are readily available and may be planted outdoors when all danger of frost is over. However, if the weather is too unpredictable, it is best to start the seed in a hotbed. Sow the seed in a rich, sandy loam and in small pots from which the small plants may be easily turned out. As with other hotbed plants, gradually allow the plants to become accustomed to the colder, open air. Transplant when 2 inches tall, and allow at least a foot space between rows to make constant cultivation possible without injury to the delicate plants. Keep free from weeds at all times. Within 4 months in a warm season the herb will blossom and mature and the seed be ready for harvesting.

Harvesting: Seed. As soon as the tops wither and the seed lose their dark green color, the plants may be cut by hand and placed on a white cloth on a screen to dry in a shady, airy spot. The seed may then be rubbed out by hand or beaten out with sticks as is done on the cumin plantations along the Mediterranean. When the seed are dry, remove all extra sprigs and extraneous leaves and be sure the clean seed are completely dry. If not, allow to dry out well. Store seed in tightly closed containers ready for use.

DILL, *Anethum graveolens,* was used by the ancient Greeks and Romans to weave pungently fragrant garlands as crowns for the foreheads of their conquering heroes. Their poets sang its praises and grew lyrical over the feathery beauty of the dill branches forever springing anew in the gardens of Athens and Rome.

Wreaths of the dark, dull yellow dill flowers were woven into decorations for the Romans' banquet halls. There the aromatic and half-unpleasant fragrance of the flowers seemed to cleanse the heavy air and permeate the spacious, stuffy halls with the herb's spicy and peculiar freshness.

The ancient Greeks treasured *aneton* or dill beyond many of the other herbs, and it was among their favorites as a condiment. It is believed now that the "anise" mentioned in the Bible as a tithe of the Pharisees was in reality the GREEK DILL.

Characteristics: Annual, more than 3 feet tall, with long wisps of bluish-green leaves which look somewhat like the feathery tips of the fennel plant. The minute yellow flowers grow in umbels which spread to look like miniature umbrellas. Dill is easily grown in temperate climates, in fairly good soil, and when protected from the wind. Excellent along the north side of the garden against a stone wall.

The seed are the dried fruit of the herb, and the tiny, oval, brown mericarps are rarely more than ⅓ inch long. The scent and taste are both warm and sharp.

Uses: Fresh leaves and tips. The tender young herb is used in seasoning countless varieties of foods such as *cheeses, fish, eggs, meats, pickles, poultry, salad dressings, vegetables,* and *soups.* When dried, the herb loses some of its flavor.

Seed. Both the whole and the ground seed are equally delicious as flavoring in *pies, vegetables, soups,* and *gravies.* The oil is a valuable industrial product used chiefly as a scent in soaps and perfumes.

Cultivating: The herb grows easily in any moderately rich soil, and though it spreads and self-sows readily, the delicate roots do not lend themselves to transplanting. Therefore, seed should be planted where the herb will be allowed to stand. The north side of the garden is best so that the tall, willowy stems will not shade the other garden plants. Plant seed in the early spring in rows 18 inches apart, using about 20 seed to a foot. The young seedlings may be thinned to stand 8 inches apart, and the herb should be well weeded. Stakes will be necessary after the plant is about 18 inches high, otherwise the slender stem will be blown over by the wind.

Germination takes place in from 10 to 15 days if seed are sown in the spring. Fall-sown seed will germinate the following spring.

If a continuous supply of tender young sprigs and leaves is

wanted all season, resow at intervals of every 3 weeks after the first planting.

Harvesting: Herb. The fresh green leaves are ready to use about 6 weeks after planting. The fruiting umbels are ready to harvest for seed just as soon as they are fully developed but not brown. These fruiting tops may be used both fresh and dried.

Seed. To dry the umbels, cut and place them on a very fine screen or tray in a dark, dry room for several days. The seed are then easily stripped by rubbing the umbels between the palms of the hands. Store in tightly closed containers for use as needed.

Whole spray. The stems are cut and tied in small bundles immediately. Then they should be hung up to dry in a warm, airy place out of the sun so they may retain as much of the natural color as possible.

FENNEL or **SWEET FENNEL,** *Foeniculum vulgare,* var. *dulce,* has one of the richest histories of any of the herbs known to mankind. From a symbol of flattery to an emblem of heroism, fennel has run the gamut of legendry and superstition since centuries before the beginning of the Christian Era. For more than 3,000 years this exotic, spicy herb has been the subject of scientist and poet alike. Shakespeare, who mentioned so many fragrant herbs in his plays, gave credit to the superstition that whoever might eat fennel would have a clearer vision.

Like the garlands of dill with which the Greeks and Romans decorated their heroes, fennel was also a symbol of victory with them. The Romans, too, not only crowned their warriors with fennel, but enjoyed the pungent sweetness of the stalks of fennel, which they ate raw. The Italians today, no matter where they may wander, are still faithful to both the fennel plant and the seed.

Fennel was taken from its native Mediterranean habitat to other parts of the world; and from its cultivation in many of the earliest European monasteries the herb gradually found its way into Egypt, France, India, Persia, Japan, Switzerland, and Central Europe. As early as the fourteenth century fennel had become a household word, and when it reached England a century later it was grown as a popular potherb.

The fennel seed were used medicinally for many centuries before they became known as a culinary seasoning. It was not until the beginning of the fourteenth century that these seed were used in northern Europe to flavor foods.

Characteristics: Plant. A hardy perennial grown as an annual. All the varieties of fennel have a feathery foliage of beautiful bright green, and the umbelliferous clusters of tiny yellow flowers appear during the second season and mature in the fall of the year. Fennel grows easily and requires very little cultivation. Always plant the tall varieties along the north side of the garden to prevent shading other plants.

COMMON or WILD FENNEL, *Foeniculum vulgare,* grows from 4 to 6 feet tall and should always be sheltered from the wind. The varieties of the sweet fennel are much smaller and rarely grow more than 2 feet tall. The small sweet fennel, also called CAROSELLA, has large stems flattened at the base and looks much like celery. A dwarf variety, called FINOCCHIO, has a bulbous base which is often cooked. Finocchio needs much the same cultivation and soil as celery. In all temperate climates both the common fennel and the sweet fennel are hardy perennials.

Seed. It is oblong, light chartreuse, about ¼ inch long, and somewhat resembles caraway seed. The fennel seed, however, has five tiny ridges along the oval side and is not curved as the caraway. Many of the seed have a short piece of stem attached. The ground fennel seed are light brown in color, and the flavor is deliciously sweet like that of anise or licorice.

Uses: Leaves. The fennel leaves are used to flavor such foods as *fish, salads,* and *soups.* The stems or stalks are cut and eaten raw like celery; and the root of the dwarf fennel is also eaten raw as well as boiled and seasoned like other root vegetables.

Seed. The fennel seed, crushed and ground, are used as a flavoring in *liqueurs, confections,* and as a sweetening aroma for *perfumes.* The whole seed are the delight of many bakers and add a distinctive flavor to *cakes* and *cookies.* Other foods such as *cheeses, eggs, fish, shellfish,* and *vegetables* may be delightfully seasoned with fennel seed.

Cultivating: In mild climates the seed are usually planted in the early spring; in other parts of the country, not until July. It is best to consult local seed catalogues for exact planting instructions for each variety. The dwarf varieties of fennel will grow about 2 feet tall, the others from 4 to 6 feet. Very little weeding is necessary, and the plant takes about 80 days to mature. In order to prevent shading the smaller plants, the seed should be planted along the north side of the garden at the rate of about a dozen seed to the foot. Cover seed but ½ inch and thin the young plants to at least 8 inches apart. A dozen plants are ample for the average family.

Harvesting: Leaves. The fresh leaves and tender stems may be used by carefully cutting from time to time. When the stalks are more than a foot tall and the bulbous bases about 2 inches in diameter, the dwarf fennel may be blanched by heaping soil around the stalks, as in blanching celery. About 10 days later the cutting may begin.

In mild climates the herb roots may be left in the earth all winter if carefully mulched. In other climates the roots may be dug up and stored in a cool place the same as celery.

Seed. The tops of the fruiting umbels containing the seed may be cut before the tops turn brown and shatter. Spread on a clean, fine screen and dry in a warm, shady spot. Seed may be easily rubbed out between palms of hands. Remove all stems from seed and store seed in tightly closed containers.

GARLIC, *Allium sativum,* has been grown in Syria and Egypt for thousands of years. It was one of the chief vegetables eaten by the ancient Egyptian slaves and laborers. The Chinese knew the uses of garlic more than 2,000 years B.C., and like many far more aromatic herbs, its praises were sung by the Greek poets.

The Israelites, in their agony in Egypt, learned to eat garlic evidently with great relish. For in their march in search of the land of Canaan they cried out to Moses:

> *We remember the fish, which we did eat in Egypt freely; the cucumbers, and the melons, and the leeks, and the onions, and the garlick: But now our soul is dried away.*

In the herb garden of the Benedictine monastery of St. Gall, Switzerland, garlic was one of the favored herbs, and Charlemagne grew it commercially. Today in several of our Southern states, as well as in Oregon, Texas, and California, garlic is cultivated on a large commercial scale. The herb is so generally useful, however, that its cultivation is really universal.

Characteristics: Garlic is a bulbous annual which requires approximately the same cultivation as its cousin, the onion. The bulb is made up of as many as 12 or 14 small sections or tiny bulblets called cloves. These are held together by a tissue-paper-thin skin which covers the bulb completely. The tall, flat, tapering leaves all stem from the central bulb, and the tiny white blossoms form masses of umbels.

There are three distinct varieties of garlic grown commercially: the CREOLE or AMERICAN with the clear, white skin; the ITALIAN or MEXICAN garlic with the pink sheath; and the large TAHITI bulb which sometimes measures 3 inches in diameter and is made up of but 4 or 5 very large cloves. The leaves of this variety resemble the foliage of leek.

Garlic salt is the preparation of the dried garlic clove and sodium chloride.

Garlic powder, as its name implies, is the pure dried and crushed garlic clove. The powder is highly concentrated.

Uses: Garlic is a "must" in many traditional *salad dressings* and *shellfish recipes*. It is much more popular as an epicurean flavoring than any of its relatives or near relatives. Garlic, wisely and discreetly utilized, will add a distinctive and delicate savory to many foods such as *fish, shellfish, meats, pickles, poultry, sauces,* and *soups*.

Cultivating: The garlic bulbs are separated and each clove is set into the earth as one sets onion plants. The soil should be well prepared and small beds or ridges made. There is no general or set rule as to the size of the beds or ridges. To prevent the bulb from swelling, care should be taken not to press the cloves too deeply into the earth; nor should they be set so shallow that the rain could wash them out. Set each clove base downward about 1½ or 2 inches deep, 6 inches apart, in rows spaced about 15 inches.

The beds thrive best in moderately rich, sandy soil which is moist but well drained. In the North, planting begins in the early spring; but in the South, during the fall months. Garlic should be kept fertilized and the plants cultivated and kept free from weeds. When the soil washes away from the roots, as it will occasionally, the soil should be carefully hoed up to cover them.

Harvesting: When the tops begin to turn yellow, from May to July, depending upon the locality, the herb should be pulled from the earth. The bulbs, with foliage and all, should be dried in the open for several days. Then remove any extra loose sheaths and cut off the foliage. If the garlic is to be braided into strings as it appears in so many of the Italian markets, at least 2 inches of the foliage should be left attached to the bulbs. Store the bulbs in baskets or gunny sacks in a very dry place free from frost.

HOREHOUND, *Marrubium vulgare,* has been known chiefly as a medicinal herb over the centuries and is one of the few herbs whose uses have changed little since the discovery of its healing qualities early in Greek and Roman history. Many ailments of the throat and lungs were treated with this bitter herb, and Pliny has listed the medicinal virtues of horehound in his writings.

It was not until the nineteenth century that horehound candy became a great wintertime favorite. And only recently have the tender leaves and flowers been used as a rare culinary seasoning. The bitterness of the herb invests it with a certain element of risk, but because of its grayish-green beauty, horehound remains an important garden herb.

Characteristics: Hardy perennial, about 18 inches tall; inclined to spread and form a bush. The grayish-green, oval leaves are crinkly and downy. The whorls of tubular, white flowers grow in the upper axils close to the stems and the leaves.

Horehound will grow in practically all climates and has spread as a weed in America from the Atlantic to the Pacific coasts. In the garden it has a tendency to winterkill and grows best in a dry, sunny spot. Makes an attractive gray edge if kept from spreading too much.

Uses: The young tender leaves and flowers of the horehound herb are used in foods such as *cakes, cookies, candies, sauces, meat stews,* and in *herb teas.*

Cultivating: Horehound grows well in any dry, light, poor soil. It is propagated by seed or root divisions. The seed may be planted in a sunny spot early in the spring in drills covered with an inch of soil. Plants should be spaced from 8 to 10 inches apart so stems cannot grow too large, for the plant has a tendency to fall over and spread. The smaller stems are far more tender and have a much better flavor.

Horehound is lovely as a gray border, and if used as such the seed or young plants should be reset every other season since the plant is subject to winterkilling.

If desired, the seed may be started in cold frames and then transplanted to the garden when all danger of frost is past.

Harvesting: Cut the small stems close to the ground. If the stems are large and the plant tall, only the top, tender part of the stems should be cut. Cutting should take place just before flowering, and the herb dried on screens in a shady place so the herb will retain its natural color. Select only the choicest, clean leaves and stems and store them in tightly closed opaque containers until used.

HORSERADISH, *Rorippa armoracia* or *Radicula armoracia,* is a member of the mustard family which has been a culinary favorite for more than 3,000 years. The Greeks used horseradish as a flavoring more than a thousand years before the time of Christ, and it was one of the herbs in use in England long before the Romans introduced the English to the luxuries of saffron and other rare herbs and spices.

This fiery herb has since found its way into all parts of the world and now grows wild as far north as the arctic regions and Iceland. Horseradish thrives best in the North Temperate climates and in the cool, high altitudes of the tropical countries.

For countless years horseradish has been cultivated in Asia, Africa, England, France, Germany, Holland, India, and practically all tropical countries. The commercial production of the herb in the United States is confined to the North Temperate sections of the country, principally in Connecticut, Massachusetts, Michigan, Missouri, New Jersey, Ohio, Pennsylvania, and Washington.

Characteristics: Perennial, with large, luxuriant, very dark green foliage. The edible long, white, fibrous root varies in size from 1 to 2 inches in diameter and from 6 to 12 inches in length. Requires moist soil and humidity for best results.

Uses: The young tender leaves of the herb may be used in *salads.* The freshly ground root, blended with distilled vinegar, is a popular condiment and is used extensively with *roasts,* in *salad dressings,* and unusual *herb sauces.*

Cultivating: This herb grows best in a rich, deep, mellow, moist soil in a cool, humid climate and is propagated from root cuttings. These are planted as early as possible in the spring. The roots are cut off square at the top and sloping at the bottom so that there is no doubt which is the lower end for insertion into the earth. The cuttings are set about 5 inches deep, 2 feet apart, in rows spaced 30 inches. The earth is cultivated until the large leaves spread and cover all the intervening space; then it is no longer necessary.

The roots may be lifted twice during the season. The first may be taken from the earth when the largest leaves are about 8 or 10 inches long. In lifting the roots, the soil is carefully removed, the crown end of the set is raised, and all but the best sprout or crown of leaves is removed. Any small roots which have started near the top or sides are rubbed off, leaving only the strong ones at the bottom. The set is returned to its normal position and the soil replaced. About 6 weeks later the process may be repeated, and the result is a large, smooth root free from rough spots and tiny side roots.

Harvesting: Usually late in October or early November is the best time for harvesting. The tops are cut 3 or 4 days before the roots are dug. When taken from the soil, all small roots are trimmed off. The large roots are brushed clean and stored in cool cellars, barns, outside pits, or cold storage, as other root vegetables are, until ready for use.

Roots should not be exposed to the light during the time they are in storage, for the light turns the roots green.

HYSSOP, *Hyssopus officinalis,* is mentioned so often in biblical history in connection with agony and suffering that we may have lost sight of the real meaning of the word. Its literal translation from the Greek means "aromatic herb."

Although the ancients never used hyssop as a culinary herb, they knew its medicinal and cleansing values. Moses, Solomon, and also David in the Psalms sang of the hyssop, and it was one of the chief herbs used in the ceremonies of repentance and purification.

Our garden hyssop of today is probably not the same hyssop of Palestine, but we believe it to be a plant which came from southern Europe. It had a special place in the formal gardens of Virginia, where hyssop hedges were popular during the eighteenth century. Today hyssop continues to be not only a favorite garden herb but also one of the most profuse of the herbs found growing wild along both coasts of America.

Characteristics: A hardy perennial, almost evergreen. Average height is about 2 feet, and the narrow dark green leaves have a spicy, minty taste and aroma. The flower spikes are set close to the stems, and there are three species of this handsome true hyssop which take their names from the colors of the blossoms. The BLUE HYSSOP has the dark blue blossoms; the PINK HYSSOP, *Hyssopus rubra,* has the pink petals; and the WHITE HYSSOP, or *Hyssopus alba,* is named for its snow-white flowers.

Uses: Tender young leaves are used to flavor *fruit cocktails, rich, fat fish, game, meats, pies, salads, soups,* and *stews.* It's chief industrial use is as a scent in *toilet waters* and as a flavoring in the liqueur, Chartreuse.

Cultivating: Hyssop seed are readily available at seed stores, and the herb is very easy to grow. Plant the seed in a light, well-drained soil in a spot which is partially shady. Thin the seedlings so that the mature plants are spaced at least a foot apart. Keep carefully cut back after the first blossoms appear. If this is done the plants will continue to bloom and new, tender, minty leaves may be cut continuously for use. Hyssop may also be propagated by root divisions and cuttings.

Harvesting: For drying, it is always best to select the tender young flowering tips. Cut the herb in the early morning as soon as the dew has evaporated but before the sun has become too hot. Place the young stems on a tray or screen over which a clean white cloth has been carefully stretched. Dry in the shade, or indoors where there is plenty of air circulating. Turn the herb gently occasionally, and when completely dried store in tightly covered containers until ready to use. See also Chapter Five, "Drying Herbs."

JUNIPER BERRIES, *Juniperus communis.* Even this shrub of the wilderness has its legend in history. And the dried, ripe fruit of the common juniper are used in such epicurean ways that it seemed impossible to omit the herb from this volume, though perhaps none of us will ever try to transplant and cultivate this hardy bush of the woodlands in a small garden.

Tradition says that when the Virgin Mary and the Christ child were fleeing from King Herod into the land of Egypt they sought refuge behind the spreading branches of the juniper bush and were protected from the fury of the despotic ruler.

Characteristics: Shrub. The juniper of the family *Pinaceae* has an erect trunk and its sprawling, evergreen branches are covered with a shreddy bark. The small awl-shaped leaves are from ¼ to ½ inch long and have sharp, prickly points.

Flowers. During May and June the flowers appear on separate twigs. The male flowers blossom in short catkins and the female in short cones.

Fruit. The berrylike round fruit ripens in October of the second year. It is dark purple with a pale blue overbloom. Each fruit holds 3 seed embedded in a brownish pulp. When dried the seed are a darker purple and their taste is slightly bitter, with a sweetish, almost spicy aroma.

The juniper shrub or tree is found growing wild on most of the dry, sterile hills of the Northern Hemisphere: from Canada south to New Jersey, west to Nebraska, and in the Rocky Mountains south to New Mexico. It is also found in Central America, northern Asia, and Europe.

Uses: The berries are used in great quantities commercially in the manufacture of *gins, liqueurs,* and *bitters.* However, certain blends of *pickling spices* will contain the berries, and their culinary uses are legion. The piquant flavor of the juniper berry is used to add a most unusual seasoning quality to such foods as *game, meats, poultry, sauces, soups, stew,* and *marinades.*

Cultivating: Wild in the greater part of the Northern Hemisphere.

Harvesting: Late in October, when the berrylike fruits in the catkins and cones have matured and ripened, the twigs may be broken off. The seed is then extracted from the surrounding pulp. Place the seed or berries on a clean tray and allow to dry slowly in a cool, dry place. Store dried berries in tightly closed opaque containers ready for use.

LAVENDER, *Lavandula vera.* The early history of this strikingly lovely, fragrant herb with its long, slender foliage is lost in antiquity.

In the records which have been left us, however, we read that the Phoenicians, Egyptians, Greeks, and Romans all loved the sweet scent of lavender. They used the flowering tips and the foliage as perfume and burned the lavender twigs as incense. We believe that the herb is native to southern Europe, especially along the Mediterranean coast.

The Greeks used lavender extravagantly in their sacrifices to the gods. They tenderly wrapped their virgins in lavender and laurel branches before burning them as sacrificial offerings to appease the angry gods.

The emperors and kings of France perfumed their silks and satins with the sweetness of the then incredibly expensive herb. Gradually, as lavender was cultivated more generally and it became more plentiful and less expensive, its fragrant flowers were used to perfume the linens in practically every household. Its refreshing, almost permanent perfume soon became a symbol of cleanliness and purity.

The stimulating aroma of the flowers was discovered as an antidote to dizziness long centuries ago. Today we still use the refreshing effects of lavender salts as an agreeable preventive for fainting. Many an eighteenth- and nineteenth-century maiden is said to have been revived by a whiff of lavender salts.

Characteristics: Among the three most cultivated of the lavenders are the true or ENGLISH LAVENDER, the FRENCH or *Lavandula stoechas,* and the SPIKE LAVENDER, *Lavandula spica.*

English lavender is a hardier perennial than the French lavender. The blunt leaves of the English species are narrow and a bluish-green in color. The plant in mild climates may attain a height of 3 feet or more. The fragrant blue flowers grow on spikes on the square stems and are grouped in whorls of 6 or more. English lavender spreads rapidly unless carefully pruned.

The long, narrow leaves of the French lavender are grayish-green, and the scented flowers, also growing on spikes, are a rich dark purple. This lavender is a smaller shrub, about a foot high, and thrives best in the warmer climates. Its delicate gray foliage is unusually attractive in the garden, and if taken indoors during the winter months, in the colder climates, it can be set out again in the springtime.

The small, shrubby spike lavender is popular in the Northern states. Its slender, oblong leaves are hoarier than the English lavender, and the flower stems reach high above the body of the plant. The heavily perfumed flowers of spike lavender blossom at the tips of the tall stems.

Uses: The flowering tips are used commercially chiefly in *perfumes, soaps, herbal tobaccos,* and *scented sachets.* However, in the new culinary experiments the petals of the flowers and the young tips of the herb are being used as flavorings in *beverages* and *jellies.* See also Chapter Nine, "Herb and Spice Sweet Scents and Sachets."

Cultivating: Lavender thrives best in a sunny dry soil, and after it gets a really good start can be a most satisfactory and beautiful herb. In rock gardens, and especially along the top of a stone wall, lavender will spread and grow luxuriantly. In the beginning the plant may be quite temperamental since the seed germinate slowly. When the seed is planted in some of our Northern gardens in the late fall just before the ground freezes, germination begins early in the following spring, and by the middle of the summer the strong seedlings are ready to be transplanted.

When the young plants are purchased from a nursery they may be set out early in the spring after all danger of frost is past. Rooted cuttings may also be set out at this time. The soil should be light, dry, well prepared, and the young plants placed in a sunny, well-drained section of the garden. Set them from 12 to 15 inches apart in rows separated at least a foot so the plants can be easily weeded.

Not many blossoms should be cut the first year. It is best to prevent the plant from blossoming in order to allow it to grow luxuriant and bushy. Then for the 3 years following it will blossom well. If well protected from the cold and dampness, the plant will not winterkill even in the northern climates. If there is any uncertainty, however, it is best to take the plants indoors and care for them there or in a greenhouse. New plants should replace the older ones at least every 4 years.

Harvesting: As the buds begin to open or when in full bloom, the flowering tops are cut and placed on a tray or a screen over which a clean white cloth has been carefully stretched. The tops are then dried in the shade, and the flowers are easily stripped from the stems by hand as soon as they are thoroughly dried. If preferred, flowering tops may be loosely tied in a cheesecloth and hung to dry in a shady spot. Store dried flowers in tightly covered containers until ready to use.

When the flowering tops are used to produce oil, they are distilled at once without drying.

LEEK, *Allium porrum,* is one of the milder members of the onion family whose natural habitat has been obscured in history. Botanists have been unable to determine its actual native source. The WILD LEEK, *Allium amelophrasum,* is still found in the fields and meadows of Europe and Asia from Siberia to the southern Mediterranean coasts. This species also grows wild in England and Wales. Another wild species, the *Allium tricoccum,* flourishes in the woods of the North American continent from New Brunswick to the state of Iowa.

Undoubtedly it was the ancient Egyptians and Chinese who cultivated and developed the herb as a food. The Romans during the time of Pliny discovered the medicinal qualities of leek. They also used the raw, tender green shoots in the elaborate salads served to precede their Lucullan banquets.

Ever since the Welsh soldiers wore leeks in their caps when fighting the Saxons in A.D. 640, the leek has been a legendary symbol of honorable service. And to this day many a Welshman, on the first of March, will wear a *boutonnière* of fresh leek in honor of David, the patron saint of Wales. It was said that he had once done penance by fasting on leek, which he himself had found in the fields.

Characteristics: Large, onionlike, succulent plants with flat, broad green leaves which branch out from the long stalks. The lower part of the stalk is blanched about 3 or 4 inches, and the diameter of the oblong lower white end is from ½ to 1½ inches, depending upon when the herb has been pulled from the earth. Leeks can be used any time after they are as large as green onions or scallions. The aroma of the herb is very strong, but the flavor is mild and sweet.

Uses: Both the fresh green tops and the blanched roots may be used as flavoring in *soups* and *salads* when a very mild onion flavor is desired. The whole herb with the tender part of the green top is prepared as a vegetable, and leek is the base for the famous French *Vichyssoise.* The French peasants are especially fond of whole leeks. In fact, the herb has become known in France as "the poor man's asparagus."

Cultivating: Like onions, leeks may be started from seed in seedbeds, or indoors in cold frames, or in the open. If sown from seed in the early spring, small trenches about 8 inches deep should be prepared and the seed then covered with but ½ inch of soil. As the tiny plants grow they should be thinned to 6 inches apart and in rows spaced 18 inches. The trenches should be gradually filled in with earth as the plant develops so that the growing stalks become blanched.

Harvesting: Dig the plants with roots and reset them in boxes of moist soil as in storing celery. If the climate is mild and there is no danger of frost and freezing, the plants may be left in the ground and used as needed.

LOVAGE or **LOVE PARSLEY,** *Levisticum officinale,* is among the historical list of herbs grown by the Benedictine monks at St. Gall, near the shores of the shimmering blue of Lake Constance in Switzerland.

Lovage is native to the Italian Alps and southern France, so it is a foregone conclusion, as well as history, that Charlemagne also grew this stunning, tropical-looking plant in his gardens.

Both the Greeks and the Romans used all parts of the plant: the leaves, the seed, the sweet roots, and the large stalks or stems. Like many of the better-known herbs, lovage found its way to America with our New England ancestors. They chewed bits of the dried root as they did cinnamon bark and coriander seed to chase away the ennui of long and tedious sermons.

A wild species called SEA LOVAGE or SCOTTISH LOV-AGE grows along the northern Atlantic seacoast north of the state of New York. It is the same species as that which is known in the Isle of Skye, where the Scottish fisherfolk cook the young, aromatic leaves and eat them as greens.

Characteristics: Plant. Tall, hardy perennial from 5 to 7 feet high with large pale green and heavy leaves resembling the foliage of celery. The coarse leaves grow away from the round, hollow stalk. Umbels of greenish-yellow flowers appear early in the spring and will grow in bright open sunshine with very little care. Place lovage in the garden where it will not cast a shade over the smaller plants. Blossoms during June and July.

Root. Thick, dark brown, with numerous fibers or offsets.

Seed. Small like caraway seed, slightly curved, ribbed on the outer side, smooth on the inside, with a sweet, aromatic taste.

Uses: Leaves. Young tender leaves, either fresh or dried, *may be used as celery is used* to flavor *soups, sea foods, chowders, salads, sauces,* and *stews.* Roots. Used chiefly for the aromatic oil which is extracted and utilized as flavoring in some *tobacco blends* and *perfumes.* Seed. Used both whole and ground as aromatic seasoning in such foods as *cakes, candies, game, meat pies, meat stews, roasts,* and *salads.* Stems. When blanched, may be eaten raw as celery.

Cultivating: The seed are sown indoors in late September as celery seed is, and the tiny plants are set in the garden early in the following spring after all danger of frost has passed. A bright, open, sunny spot is the best location, and the soil should be rich and moist. The tall, beautiful plant makes an exceedingly lovely background in the garden, and the plants should be spaced about 3 feet in rows at least a foot apart. If only sufficient plants for family use are desired, 3 or 4 will be ample. The plant thrives easily, and very little care is necessary. If the herb is to be used as celery, the stems should be blanched with earth as in blanching celery.

Harvesting: Roots. The roots may be dug in October of the second or third year after the plants have been set in the open. The good offsets may be trimmed from the roots and used to renew or enlarge the garden. When roots are to be dried for use they should be washed thoroughly, cut into slices about ½ inch thick, and very carefully spread on a white cloth stretched over a screen. Dry in a warm, shady spot where there is a good circulation of air. Turn pieces of root at intervals so drying will be uniform. When completely dried, store in tightly covered opaque containers until ready for use.

Seed. If seed are to be harvested, proceed in the same way as when harvesting caraway seed. The fruiting umbels of the lovage should be cut from the plant before they begin to shatter so that none of the seed are lost.

Stems. If lovage has been blanched as celery, the small tender stems may be cut and eaten as a vegetable.

MARIGOLD or **POT MARIGOLD,** *Calendula officinalis,* with its aromatic petals of bitter taste and bright golden color, has vied with the sunflower in literary popularity. Perhaps it is because both these midsummer blossoms follow or turn with the sun that the critics have wondered if sometimes one flower was not mistaken for the other. However, Shakespeare quite definitely must have meant the marigold in the lines of Perdita in *The Winter's Tale,* Act IV, Scene 4:

> *Here's flowers for you;*
> *Hot lavender, mints, savory, marjoram;*
> *The marigold, that goes to bed wi' the sun*
> *And with him rises weeping: these are flowers*
> *Of middle summer, and I think they are given*
> *To men of middle age.*

And could there be any mistaken identity as we read those exquisite lines of Keats as he describes the marigold reopening its petals in the freshness of early morning? He described its golden beauty as making one lighthearted:

I stood tip-toe upon a little hill,
The air was cooling, and so very still,
. . . I was light hearted,
And many pleasures to my vision started . . .
Open afresh your round of starry folds,
Ye ardent marigolds!
Dry up the moisture from your golden lids
For great Apollo bids
That in these days your praises should be sung
On many harps, which he has lately strung.

Or again as we recall "Believe Me, If All Those Endearing Young Charms," which Thomas Moore gave us in the early nineteenth century, can there be any doubt but that he was singing not of the marigold but of another *asteraceous* plant in:

No, the heart that has truly loved never forgets,
But as truly loves on to the close,
As the sunflower turns to her god when he sets
The same look which she turned when he rose!

Delving back into the time of the Romans, we find in their culinary history the simple marigold vying with the fabulous saffron. When foods were colored and flavored with the powdered stigmas of the exotic saffron flower it was an indication of great wealth and power. The masses couldn't afford to buy this "pure gold" and so they discovered for themselves that the fragrance of the powdered marigold petals was an excellent substitute. History tells us that even the Romans used marigold powder as a substitute saffron flavoring when they were in Britain and found it practically impossible to secure saffron.

As the English continued the uses of marigold petals and powder the French began to flavor their foods with the golden powder and discovered that its subtle seasoning qualities were as valuable as the attractive coloring it gave to cakes and cookies.

Marigold was among the first herbs which the colonists brought with them to New England, where its beautiful yellow and orange flowers are still a favorite.

Characteristics: Hardy annual, grows from 1 to 2 feet high, depending upon geographical location. Will grow in a variety of soils, but rich loam will give best results. Blossoms early and will continue blossoming all summer. Attracts bees. Green pinnate leaves curl slightly and have a light, soft, fuzzy surface.

Oval golden-yellow and orange aromatic petals are arranged around the circular flower heads like those of daisies and sunflowers.

Uses: Fresh petals and the marigold powder lend an exotic and delicate flavor to many foods such as *sea-food stews* and *chowders, game,* and *roast meats.* See also Saffron Uses. Commercially the dried marigold petals are used in some medicines and especially in ointments.

Cultivating: The seed germinate rapidly and may be planted in moderately rich soil early in the spring. The rows should be about 18 inches apart and the seedlings transplanted to stand about a foot apart.

Harvesting: The plants blossom early and continue to bloom all summer. The flowers may be gathered every few days and carefully dried on a large canvas in a warm, dry, shady place. The flowers should be arranged very loosely so that they do not touch each other and do not become bruised. After the flower heads are dried, the petals are carefully picked off by hand and bottled in tightly corked containers. The heads are pulverized and the powder bottled in the same way as the petals.

MARJORAM or **SWEET MARJORAM,** *Origanum marjorana L.,* is one of the more than 30 species of fragrant *origanum,* which is native to the dry, sunny, rocky hills along the Mediterranean coast.

The word *origanum* is a combination of the two Greek words, *horos,* or hill, and *ganos,* or adornment. Consequently this sweet herb has been appropriately identified through its long history as the beautiful "ornament of the hills."

Not only did the Greeks recognize the beauty of marjoram and its unusual flavoring qualities, but their physicians discovered its value as a tonic. Virgil sang the praises of the soft perfume of the fragrant leaves, and other Roman writers, from Catullus to the horticulturist Pliny, referred to the delightfully aromatic herb which covered the rocky shores along the Aegean Sea.

Both the Greeks and the Romans crowned married couples with wreaths of sweet marjoram as a symbol of the happiness which they wished for them. In India the herb is as sacred as the holy basil.

This lovely herb with its spicy taste finally reached England by the thirteenth century, where it became a great favorite in all English households. Izaak Walton refers frequently to sweet marjoram throughout the pages of his *Compleat Angler*. Of all the herbs, his highest praise goes to "sweet Margerome," which he suggests should be used by the "handful" when seasoning freshly caught fish. Since then, however, we have learned to use all herbs with a more delicate touch.

Perhaps nowhere in all the world is marjoram used more extensively than on the little island of Sicily. And the ancient city of Marjori had as its coat of arms a spray of marjoram on a field of blue. The marjoram symbolized the fragrant carpeting of the sometimes barren Sicilian hills, and the blue represented the azure seas surrounding them.

Characteristics: Many species of this lovely perennial are now cultivated all over the earth. The three most popular are perhaps the sweet marjoram, *Origanum marjorana,* the POT MARJORAM, *Origanum onites,* and the WILD MAR-JORAM, *Origanum vulgare.*

Sweet marjoram, like the other varieties, is a perennial which has to be grown as an annual in the cooler climates since it winterkills easily. The herb reaches a height of from 12 to 15 inches, has small, oval, grayish-green leaves on delicate woody stems of a slight reddish tint. The tiny white blossoms with green bracts are lovely to see in any fragrant garden. It requires early cultivation, but when once started will grow without much attention.

Pot marjoram is a smaller variety with soft green leaves and purplish flowers which add beauty and color to the garden. In the out-of-doors it will sprawl and form a thick mound if given sufficient space and will grow almost 1½ feet tall.

Uses: Both the dried and the fresh young leaves are used to flavor a great variety of foods such as *eggs, fish, game, meats, poultry, salads, sauces, soups, stews, stuffings,* and *vegetables.* The flowering tips are valuable both medicinally and industrially, especially as a scent for *soaps* and *perfumes;* and sweet marjoram is always one of the basic herbs in blends of *poultry* and *sausage seasoning.* See also Orégano.

Cultivating: The tiny seed of both the sweet marjoram and the pot marjoram are slow to germinate. It is best, therefore, to sow the seed in a cold frame or window box. When the seedlings are 2 or 3 inches high they should be transplanted early in the spring in a dry, well-drained soil which is somewhat chalky and not too rich. Keep the seedlings well shaded and protected until their growth has been established, and allow each plant at least a foot of space each way. Weed frequently during the first weeks, and as the plant develops, very little further care is required.

Marjoram may also be started from cuttings or crown divisions. To make a cutting, pull off the woody stem with the crown or heel attached and keep in wet sand until the cutting has formed roots. Then plant as for seedlings.

Harvesting: Leaves. The first tender leaves may be cut for use when the plants are but 4 or 5 inches high. Later cuttings may be made during the season as desired; and when the plants begin to bloom, they may be cut back several inches. In the late summer, when all the leaves are harvested, they are dried as other herbs by placing them on a screen in a shady, dry place where there is a good circulation of air.

If preferred, the sprigs of sweet marjoram may be dried by tying them in bunches and hanging them up in an airy, shady, warm place. When thoroughly dried, the leaves should be stripped from the stems by hand. The clean leaves should then be pulverized and stored in tightly covered opaque containers ready for use.

MINT, *Mentha,* dates back to Greek mythology, when this lowly herb was first given the botanical name of *Mentha.* This lovely aromatic plant grew in profusion in the abundant fields of Greece, and for centuries it was trampled underfoot wherever it sprang up along the ancient roadsides.

It is said that Proserpine, the beloved of Pluto, became violently jealous of a beautiful nymph called Menthe because Pluto had become so enamored of her that he was forgetful of his first love. Proserpine, filled with revengeful envy and fury, changed the woodland Menthe into the lowliest of plants so that forever after she might be trampled beneath the feet of all the mortals on this earth. If we are to believe Claudian in his *De Raptu Proserpinae* (Book iii, c. A.D. 395), even this vengeful act did not assuage the envy of the goddess Proserpine, for we read: *"Rabiem livoris acerbi nulla potest placare quies* [Nothing can allay the rage of biting envy]."

The mint was one of the favorite and most fragrant of the herbs strewn lavishly around the banquet halls of the Greeks and Romans. By the beginning of the Christian Era the value of the oil distilled from the aromatic leaves must have become noticeably enhanced, for the mint herb was named as a tithe along with the anise and cumin seed.

The mints probably were native to Hindustan, but there are no authoritative records left to us. We only know that by the beginning of the fourteenth century the herb was used with foods, and like most of the culinary seasonings used by the Romans, mint found its way to all the corners of the earth.

Today two popular varieties of the mints, PEPPERMINT, *Mentha piperita,* and SPEARMINT, *Mentha spicata,* are grown commercially on the muck lands of southern California, Michigan, northern Indiana; also in the Pacific Northwest in similar damp soils, especially in western Oregon and Washington. In the Yakima Valley, in the south-central section of Washington, home of the famous Yakima apples, peppermint is grown under irrigation, and the production has been increasing steadily. Spearmint is cultivated less extensively than the peppermint since there is a greater demand for the oil of the latter herb.

These two varieties of mints are found wild also in all damp places from Nova Scotia to Minnesota and as far south as Utah, Tennessee, and Florida.

Characteristics: The mints are hardy perennials, propagated from roots or runners, and will grow from 1½ to 2 feet tall, depending upon the variety. APPLE MINT, *Mentha rotundifolia,* is often called WOOLLY MINT because its round leaves are soft and woolly. It is the AMERICAN APPLE MINT, *Mentha gentilis variegata,* however, which is the culinary herb. Its leaves are smooth, grayish-green, with streaks of yellow, and both the aroma and taste are delicately fruity. The light purple flowers blossom in whorls on the almost square stems during the midsummer months. The apple mint is shorter than some varieties and has a tendency to spread out.

CURLY MINT, *Mentha spicata,* var. *crispata,* has dull, crinkly, wide leaves, and the plant often stands 2 feet tall at the beginning of summer. Then the hairy stems weaken and are apt to sprawl out during the later months. Slender spikes are tipped with violet-colored flowers which blossom during midsummer.

ORANGE MINT, *Mentha citrata,* is also called BERGAMOT MINT (not to be confused with bergamot or wild bergamot, *Monarda fistulosa*). The smooth leaves edged with a tinge of purple are broader than those of the more familiar peppermint, but the stems have the same reddish hue of so many of the mint varieties. The purple flowers grow at the tips of short spikes, and the whole plant has a tendency to grow in a decumbent position after it attains maturity. The orange mint is sometimes erroneously called a lavender mint because the flowers give off a faint perfume so much like the aroma of lavender. After the first quick whiff, however, the stronger fruitiness of the orange aroma becomes more pronounced.

Peppermint, *Mentha piperita,* has several common names such as BRANDY MINT, LAMB MINT, or LAMMINT, as it is sometimes spelled. There are two popular varieties of peppermint: The *Mentha piperita,* var. *vulgaris,* or BLACK PEPPERMINT, has dark green leaves tinged with purple, like those of the orange mint, but the stems are more purple and the purple flowers blossoming at the tips of long spikes are tinged with red. The *Mentha piperita,* var. *officinalis,* or the WHITE PEPPERMINT, has light green leaves and purple flowers which blossom in dense clusters at the tips of long slender spikes. The white peppermint isn't as tall as the black peppermint, but the oil distilled from its leaves is said to be the best quality produced.

Uses: Industrially the oil of the mints is used in *medicines, perfumes, toilet waters, dental preparations,* and *chewing gums.* The culinary mints such as American apple mint, orange mint, peppermint, and spearmint add their delicate flavors to an infinite variety of beverages and foods such as *fruit drinks, juleps,* and other *iced beverages; teas, vinegars,* and *jellies; soups, sauces,* and *vegetables; meats, fish, salads,* and *desserts.* The young tender leaves may be used whole, freshly minced, or dried. Many liqueurs owe their distinctive character to the flavor of the mints. Chartreuse usually contains orange mint as well as peppermint, while Benedictine and crème de menthe are flavored with the latter herb.

Cultivating: Among the several mints grown in herb gardens and used to flavor foods, perhaps the two most popular are the peppermint and spearmint. Both these mints are easily propagated by cuttings or divisions. Simply take a few runners—that is, stems with good roots—and reset them in a moist, well-drained, rich soil where there is plenty of shade. In the West, planting usually begins in early March, but the ground should always be reasonably warm and not too wet and all danger of frost should be past. The runners are laid in furrows 3 feet apart and 4 inches deep, then covered with earth and packed down.

If young plants are set out instead of the runners, these should be planted only after warm weather has arrived, in late May or June in the temperate zones. The plants should be set a foot apart in rows spaced about 3 feet. The plants require frequent cultivation and should be kept free from weeds at all times. If the mint bed becomes too crowded, thin by pulling out all runners. Spearmint spreads rapidly, and to prevent this, the young roots should be surrounded by metal strips inserted in the ground. This species of mint also grows in a pot or window box indoors.

Harvesting: As the plants continue to grow, the tiny, young leaves and sprigs may be picked and used fresh as desired. Cutting the herb at intervals helps its growth. When the herb is to be dried, cut the leaves and flowering tips before they go to seed, otherwise the plant may die. Place herb on screen or tray in warm, dry, shady spot. When thoroughly dry, strip leaves and flowers from stems. Store in tightly covered containers. When only leaves are desired, strip them from stems separately after they are well dried. Store and use as required.

MUSTARD, *Brassica sinapis,* was a wholesome favorite vegetable of the Greeks more than 2,000 years ago. The ancient Greeks cooked the tender young green leaves of the plant and ate them much as we eat mustard greens today. They, too, discovered that the powder or flour prepared from the dried seed was an excellent *condiment* with *roast meats* and *sea foods.*

Today we are so familiar with the mustard plants that grow wild throughout most of the world that we have forgotten that this peppery plant and almost common weed was once a treasured herb in the historical herb gardens of the world. Charlemagne grew mustard plants in his gardens at Aix-la-Chapelle. Shakespeare mentioned mustard as the perfect condiment in *As You Like It* and also in *The Taming of the Shrew.*

England imported most of her mustard seed from India and Russia until the price grew so prohibitive that she had to begin to cultivate it herself. Here in America, even though the wild variety is found in great profusion, the plant is extensively cultivated for its seed in Santa Barbara County, *California,* and in several of our Western states, including *Oregon, Washington, Idaho,* and *Montana.*

Characteristics: The mustard plant varies in height from 18 inches to 4 or 5 feet, and its fuzzy leaves are varied in color, according to the variety, from yellowish- to a dark green. The clusters of tiny flowers are a bright lemon yellow and each one looks like a miniature cross. The BLACK MUSTARD, *Brassica sinapis nigra,* is a hardy annual with yellowish-green leaves and grows as high as 4 feet. It will grow in practically any dry, sterile soil. However, when grown for its seed harvest, the plant requires moisture to produce a high-quality seed.

WHITE MUSTARD, *Brassica sinapis alba,* is the small mustard plant which is suitable for the vegetable garden. Never plant this herb in or near the flower garden since it resows so freely that it could become a pest in no time at all. The white mustard grows only 18 inches high, and its tender young leaves are delicious when prepared as a cooked vegetable or mixed with a green salad.

Powder or Dry Mustard or Mustard Flour. Dry mustard is the result of crushing and milling the dried seed of the mustard plant. See also later paragraphs on harvesting of mustard seed. The pure mustard flour is a pale yellow, and the flour is usually called a spice.

Seed. The infinitesimal mustard seed grow in pairs in tiny beaklike pods called siliques. Each pod holds two carpels which are separated by a tissue-thin membrane. The seed vary in size from $\frac{3}{64}$ to $\frac{3}{32}$ of an inch in diameter. The colors vary in the seed coats only and range from pale yellow to a dark reddish-brown.

Uses: Leaves. Young, tender, raw shoots in *salads;* also in *soups* and *with other cooked greens* such as *sorrel* and *spinach.*

Seed, whole. Both black and white varieties have a large commercial use in the manufacture of *oleomargarine,* some *salad oils, soaps,* and *liniments.* The whole white or yellow varieties are used chiefly as ingredients in *pickling spices* and in *sausages. Salads* and *vegetables* may also be carefully seasoned with the whole white mustard seed.

Both the black and the white seed are used in preparing pure mustard flour. This dry mustard or flour is prepared in many forms for commercial sale and has become one of the most popular of all the condiments. It may be used in any quantity, depending upon the pungency desired, to flavor *appetizers, cheeses, eggs, fish, shellfish, game, meats, poultry, salads, sauces,* and *vegetables.*

Cultivating: Mustard is definitely a plant which requires cool winds, dampness, and fogs.

The white mustard is the species which produces the foliage used in salads and as a vegetable. It is easily grown from seed and germinates quickly in a rather heavy, sandy loam. It is wise to check with the state agricultural experiment stations concerning commercial cultivation, since both local climate and soil greatly influence the quality of the herb.

Harvesting: Leaves. The young green leaves are cut in the same way as garden spinach as soon as the plant reaches the desired size. Naturally, the smaller leaves are more tender than the older ones and far less peppery or pungent.

Seed. If seed are desired, the pods are allowed to develop fully and are cut while still closed and not completely ripe. If they were allowed to stand until fully ripe, the pods would shatter and all the tiny seed would be lost. Therefore, as soon as the pods are filled with seed and before they open, the plant is harvested. This usually begins in the month of August. The plants are cut with a mower, then dried as sheaves of grain in windrows, and threshed with a pickup harvester after the sun has dried the herb thoroughly.

The dried mustard seed are crushed to remove the hulls. The seed are then placed in bags in a hydraulic press, where about 20 per cent of the oil is extracted. The resulting mustard cakes are dried and put through a crusher, and from there through the mill to be powdered.

The first run of the mill is the true mustard flour which we call dry or ground mustard. The second grinding through the mill is often a mixture of yellow and brown mustard bran. The product of the third grinding is a plaster mustard or mustard cake. This contains both the mustard flour and the ground hulls of the seed.

The best brown seed comes from the southeast coast of Italy and the island of Sicily. However, the California brown seed is practically free from weed and is infinitely cleaner than the imported brown seed. The best grade of yellow seed comes from England, Holland, Germany, and Austria.

NASTURTIUM, *Tropaeolum majus,* is one of the brilliant garden plants which has been used also as an herb for centuries.

The nasturtium had been called WATER CRESS and IN-DIAN CRESS until early in the sixteenth century, when the Spanish physician, Nicholas Monardes, gave the tall peppery

Tropaeolum majus the name of nasturtium. Literally it means "to twist the nose."

The Orientals used the petals of the flowers in teas and exotic salads as they did the jasmine flower, and the custom is being revived here. The French, also, will often mix a few of the piquant nasturtium leaves in a combination green salad.

Characteristics: The common wild variety grows in running water with branching stems from 1 to 2 feet long. The leaves are elliptic and grow in pairs of from 3 to 7 on a stem. Their flowers are small and white.

The dwarf varieties, developed and cultivated in our gardens, are bushy and low. Their leaves may be elliptic or heart-shaped and their bell-shaped flowers of brilliant hues.

Uses: Both the delicate young foliage and the petals of the flowers are rare, exotic, and decorative additions to the flavor and the appearance of foods such as *canapés* and *salads*.

The seed and the seed pods are used as seasoning in *mixed pickles*. They are also pickled and used as a substitute for capers in seasoning *foods* and *sauces*.

Cultivating: This tender annual grows well in a light, moderately rich soil mixed with sand, and the plants thrive on sunshine and plenty of water. The seed are sown early in the springtime, as soon as all danger of frost is over. The seedlings should be thinned to stand at least 8 inches apart for the dwarf variety, and about a foot apart for the taller.

Harvesting: The young, tender leaves and stems with their peppery, pungent flavor may be used when but half grown. Later the petals of the flowers may be used alone or in combination with the small leaves and stems.

ONION, *Allium cepa,* is one of the oldest of all our cultivated herbs. It is believed to have originated in Asia, and from there its history has been one of favor and glory. During the time of Homer the humble pungent onion was considered an herb of rare delicacy. Pliny wrote that there were many varieties cultivated in Italy, and even today, though its cousin the garlic bulb is more popular, the onion is one of the most important ingredients in Italian cookery. See also Chives, Garlic, Leek, and Shallots.

Characteristics: An herb sensitive to weather and insects, but easily grown if the right variety is chosen for the particular locality. The sweet Bermuda types such as RED CREOLE and WHITE CREOLE should be planted only in the lower South. Farther north in the middle part of the United States, where the winter sowing of seed is feasible for early transplanting in the spring, the sweet Spanish onions thrive well. Varieties suitable in the North are the various types of globe onions, such as the YELLOW GLOBE, SOUTHPORT RED GLOBE, SOUTHPORT WHITE GLOBE, and WHITE PORTUGAL. Only in the more northerly states and in high altitudes will the spring sowing of seed give good results. In our garden in the Pacific Northwest it was quite easy to grow beautiful onions, free from diseases and insects, from an early spring planting of seed. Fresh seed should be obtained each year, however, for the tiny seed deteriorate very quickly.

The flavors of the various types differ. A globe type of onion called the PRIZETAKER is milder than the Yellow Globe. The SOUTHPORT YELLOW GLOBE is a popular commercial type, more pungent than the Southport White Globe. The SPANISH and BERMUDA varieties are among the sweetest.

SCALLIONS are the tender, young seedlings of onions when the bulb has not yet formed and the layers of skin are thin. They taste mild and sweet and are used in cooking when a more delicate flavor is desired than that which the mature onion gives.

Uses: As a culinary herb, the onion is perhaps the most universally popular. Its seasoning qualities are known the world over, and one may achieve any degree of desired pungency by using very little or much. Both the bulbs and the tops of the seedlings known as scallions are used fresh only. The other mature onions are always used after being well dried. The flavor of the white varieties is milder than that of either the red or yellow onions. Onion salt and onion powder are concentrated forms of the dehydrated herb and should be very sparingly used.

Use onions as desired with *appetizers, cheeses, eggs, fish, game, shellfish, meats, salads, sauces,* and in combination *with other vegetables.*

Cultivating: Onions may be grown from seed or from tiny bulb sets. If propagated by using seed, they may be started in a small seedbed early in the spring and then transplanted when the bulbs are from ½ to 1 inch in diameter. Set the bulbs at least 3 inches apart in rows separated about 10 inches. Practically all varieties of onions thrive best in a rich, moist, rather loose soil.

If the seed are planted in the place where the onions will be allowed to mature, the seedlings should be thinned out to give each bulb at least 3 inches of space. Sow the seed ½ inch deep in rich soil early in the spring. Tiny green leaves will appear in about 2½ months.

Much time and labor are saved if the onion is propagated by setting out the tiny onion sets. The plants set out in April will become scallions in about 3 weeks and full-grown onions by the middle of July.

Harvesting: Scallions. When the seedlings are thinned and the tiny bulb is just beginning to form, the small green onion or scallion is delicious when eaten raw. These young seedlings may be pulled as desired. The preferred size for use is when the bulb is no more than ½ inch in diameter.

Mature onions. Late summer or early fall in the North is harvesting time for the mature plant; or when the tops of the plants have toppled over. The plants are pulled from the earth, spread out on a hard surface, and exposed to the sun for 2 or 3 days. Then the tops are cut off and the bulbs are brought indoors and placed in a dry, airy spot. When thoroughly dry they may be kept all winter in a dry cellar where there is plenty of air and the temperature doesn't fall below 36° F.

ORÉGANO is still to be given its botanical name. Though some of our Mexican, Spanish, and Italian neighbors refer to it as wild marjoram, our botanists tell us that orégano is a species separate and apart from the other culinary marjorams. What its botanical identification may be eventually is a matter of interesting conjecture and stimulating research among our gardeners and botanists alike. However, they all agree that it belongs to the *Labiatae,* mint, family.

Characteristics: Orégano is a beautiful leafy perennial. In the colder climates the herb is treated as an annual. Its lovely oval gray-green leaves, about ½ inch long, are warmly pungent like the marjorams.

The orégano herb may grow 3 feet high in the warmer climates, and the large clusters of pale purplish-pink flowers are attractive to the bees. Orégano will grow into a lovely hedge which blossoms throughout late June, July, and August.

Uses: Leaves. Freshly minced or the dried crushed leaves may be used in many of the same ways as marjoram. However, since the flavor of orégano is so much more pungent than marjoram, care and judgment are necessary in order to achieve the best possible culinary effects. The herb adds an intriguing taste to such foods as *vegetable-juice cocktails, fish* and *shellfish salads, game, meats,* and *poultry.* See also Marjoram or Sweet Marjoram.

Powdered orégano. Used very cautiously in *sauces, soups,* and *shellfish aspic salads.* Truly epicurean.

Cultivating: Orégano plants may be started from seed cuttings or crown divisions. The seed are tiny and should be started in a cold frame or window box and covered with a very thin layer of fine soil. When the seedlings are 2 or 3 inches high they may be transplanted out of doors as soon as all danger of frost is past. They should be spaced at least a foot or more apart to allow ample room for the bush, and the soil should be rich and moist. The herb is easily grown in many sections of the country. In the Northern states it is necessary to cultivate it as an annual, but in the South and on the West Coast it thrives both as an annual and as a perennial.

Harvesting: When the herb begins to bloom, the tender leaves and top stems may be cut back a few inches and used as desired. Under some conditions where the herb thrives unusually well, it is possible to make two or three cuttings before the autumn frost. When orégano is cut for drying, the leaves and flowering tops should be dried as quickly as possible on a screen in the shade where there is a good circulation of air. When thoroughly dried, the leaves with some of the very small stems may be stripped from the woody stems by hand. Store the clean herb in tightly covered containers.

PARSLEY, *Petroselinum hortense,* is said to have originated on the island of Sardinia. And the pastoral poems of the ancient Sicilians and Greeks refer to the beautiful dark green herb over and over again. We read that the Greeks crowned their heroes of the Nemean and Isthmian games with garlands of parsley, and Greek lovers made wreaths to present to their beloved ones as expressions of true affection.

The Romans, too, used garlands to crown their victorious athletes, and their banquet tables were decorated with sumptuous parsley garlands to absorb the fumes of too much imbibing. But in addition to these festive uses the Romans prized the herb highly for its aromatic flavor in sauces and other foods.

Perhaps no other herb has ever been used in as many ways. Its almost fadeless green may have covered Anacreon's grave as it once had decorated his victorious head. For the ancient Greeks also used parsley to form funeral wreaths and planted it profusely that it might become a green, velvety carpet over the mounds of newly dug graves.

Parsley was one of the favorite herbs in the monastery garden of St. Gall, and even today every little garden in Switzerland has its patch of *petersil,* as it is called in the Swiss dialect. The word is a corruption of the Greek and German word *petersilie,* which means "parsley." Pliny wrote that the name "parsley" was derived from the Greek word *petroselinon,* which means *"stone breaker."* The Greeks believed that parsley was so good and so strong in aiding troubles of the stomach that they called it by a name which described it "as strong as a stone might be."

The English, in turn, grew to love parsley, and their poets took up its praise where the Greeks and Sicilians left off. Keats, Shakespeare, John Gay, and others refer to the deep green beauty of the parsley sprigs. As it became increasingly a favorite in English kitchens, the herb was more extensively cultivated.

From England our early colonists brought it to America; and now the herb is grown in great commercial quantities in the Southwestern part of the United States, especially in California and Texas.

Characteristics: As in a majority of the biennials, a rosette of leaves appears during the first year's growth, while the flower stalks with their umbels resembling those of the dill and caraway are produced during the second year. The DOUBLE-CURLED *Petroselinum hortense,* var. *crispum,* and the MOSS-LEAVED are two of the loveliest varieties for a beautiful edging in an herb garden. The blossoms, either white or greenish, resemble Queen Anne's Lace. The FERN-LEAVED variety, *Petroselinum hortense,* var. *filicinum,* has a less vividly colored foliage and may grow as high as 10 or 12 inches, and withstands the winter cold far better than the curly varieties. The TURNIP-ROOTED PARSLEY is a most unusual herb or vegetable and is well worth cultivating for that purpose. The large root resembles a small parsnip and when cooked has a flavor equally as sweet as celery and very similar in taste.

All varieties of parsley may be grown in all parts of the world and will thrive even in climates where the soil is inclined to bake and crack. In such instances the ground should be well cultivated.

Uses: The fresh foliage of all the varieties of cultivated parsley is best known for its decorative addition to many a chef's creation. However, in a recent survey of the food content of plants indigenous to the seven Central American countries (Honduras, British Honduras, Guatemala, El Salvador, Costa Rica, Nicaragua, and Panama), parsley was among the plants studied. Dr. Hazel E. Munsell, a research associate at the nutritional biochemistry laboratories of the Massachusetts Institute of Technology, reported that in analyzing parsley this herb was found to be a source of calcium, thiamin (vitamin B-1), riboflavin (vitamin B-2), niacin, and vitamin C. Truly a very valuable food, and not merely a decoration. As seasoning, both the dried and the fresh leaves may be used in preparing *canapés, eggs, fish, shellfish, meats, poultry, salads, sauces,* and *vegetables.*

Industrially the whole parsley herb is used, especially in coloring some *wines* and *sage cheese.*

The turnip-rooted variety is used medicinally by certain pharmaceutical houses in the preparation of mild laxatives. When cultivated as a vegetable, the root is boiled and eaten much as one eats other root vegetables.

Cultivating: A rich, moist soil is needed for parsley, and since the seed germinate slowly, it is best to soak them in lukewarm water for 24 hours before planting them indoors in a cold frame. Cover only ⅛ inch deep. The seed require 4 weeks to germinate, and for this reason the English say that it goes to the devil three times before it finally comes up. The young plants may be transplanted about 6 inches apart in rows spaced one foot. In some cases one may prefer to plant the seed outdoors. If so, it may be sown on the surface and then tamped firmly with a flat board. For a thick growth, unwanted seedlings should be thinned so that the mature plants stand at least 6 inches apart; also the leaves may be clipped.

The plant blossoms during the second year. To prevent the herb from going to seed, the delicate blossoms, which look like Queen Anne's Lace, should be cut off as soon as they appear. In the fall the herb may be dug up and potted. Care should be taken to dig up as much of the root as possible, and some of the outside foliage should be cut from the plant. The potted herb is as easily taken care of as any house plant, and one may enjoy its freshness through all winter months.

Harvesting: The first tender sprigs may be cut as soon as the leaves are well formed. This usually takes place about July. From then on, the leaves with a portion of the stem may be cut as needed. To dry the leaves, the tender parts of the stems are cut from the plants and placed on a screen in a shady, dry, well-ventilated location. When thoroughly dried, they may be crushed and stored in small, tightly covered containers.

Turnip-rooted variety. When the plant has developed the enlarged root, it is dug up as carrots, parsnips, or any of the root vegetables and may be stored in the same manner for use later in the winter season.

POPPY SEED, *Papaver rhoeas,* is the dried seed of the poppy plant, which was known to the Egyptians earlier than 1500 B.C. The species cultivated for culinary use is not to be confused with the opium poppy, *Papaver somniferum.*

The Greeks, Romans, and many of the monks in most of the medieval monasteries grew the poppy for its medicinal properties. The tragic history of the opium poppy reveals greed and sordidness; but in spite of its devastating record this one-time rare and exotic flower was a love charm in the legendry of the Greeks and a symbol of peaceful sleep in Roman history.

It remained for the Dutch to develop one of the species of the poppy for its delightfully aromatic seed. Today in the Dutch province of Zeeland, the mastery of cultivating the poppy plant for its delectable walnut-flavored seed is handed down with great pride within a family from generation to generation.

Characteristics: Both the annual and the perennial varieties of poppies are easily grown from seed and will develop greater height in the more temperate and warmer regions where the climatic conditions are not too variable. This exotic flower with its green stems tinged with a blue haze has beautiful 4-petaled oyster-white blossoms tinged with blue. They may measure as much as 4 inches in diameter. The oriental poppies are more brilliantly colored and range from the deep yellows to intense crimsons. The rough, almost globular seed pods, containing hundreds of tiny seed, grow from 1 to 1½ inches in diameter.

Seed. The infinitesimal, almost cylindrical seed vary in color from a pure white to a deep blue which looks almost black, depending upon the variety of the poppy and where it is grown.

Uses: The seed are used chiefly in preparing fancy *cakes, cookies,* and *pastries.* However, recently many new culinary uses have been tested, and the nutty flavor of the oily seed adds an exciting new taste to *canapés, sweet vegetables, fruit salads,* and *sauces.* The gray poppy seed, sometimes referred to as *maw,* are usually one of the many seed found in the commercial birdseed mixtures. The oil from the crushed seed is also finding some commercial use as a *substitute* for the more expensive *olive oil.*

Cultivating: Practically all varieties of poppies are readily grown from seed. However, it is best to check soil and climatic conditions before choosing the variety. In the warm and temperate zones, where the perennials have their best growth and there is no danger of frost, one may plant either the perennials or the annuals. Where there is an uncertainty as to the evenness of the temperature, it is best to select only the annuals. All poppies are colorful and decorative in the garden, especially as an attractive border. The soil should be fairly rich, with an average amount of moisture and plenty of sunshine. Sow the seed in the exact place where the plants are to grow. The seedlings can be pulled up to allow for a spacing of about 6 inches for each plant.

Harvesting: When the flowers are allowed to go to seed the pod is cut as soon as it has turned brown but is not so dry that it will shatter. The pods are carefully dried on a screen placed in a shady, airy spot. The seed are then easily rubbed out between the palms and placed on a clean cloth until thoroughly dried. They are then ready to store in tightly covered containers.

ROSE, *Rosaceae.* In the myriad records and writings of poets, journalists, dramatists, essayists, and historians we read how the romantic charm and mystical beauty of the rose inspired them to tragedy, humor, and tenderness; romance and drama; philosophy and mysticism. All these moods and more speak to us in the words of a Byron or a Keats. The lyric beauty of this loveliest of flowers is reflected in the lines of a Swinburne or a Rosetti. A Shelley, a Wordsworth, a Marlowe, or an Arnold; a Shakespeare, a Thomas Moore, or a Wilde, a Browning, a Millay, or a Frost. All have written of the breathless glory of "the flower of Venus."

Myths and proverbs: There are countless proverbs of the rose with its thorn. One of the simplest and shortest is the old Italian one: *"Non v'è rosa senza spina* [No rose without a thorn]." A more modern version is given in the expression of Frank K. Stanton: "You git a thorn with every rose, But ain't the roses sweet?" However, Gertrude Stein said perhaps all there was to be said about this mystical symbol of life, love, and secrecy when she wrote: "A rose is a rose is a rose is a rose."

The ancient Greeks told us that the red rose came from the blood of Adonis. Centuries later this immortal myth was reiterated in those memorable lines of *The Rubáiyát:* "I sometimes think that never blows so red The rose as where some buried Caesar bled." Long before the days of the Roman conqueror, the people gloried in the perfume of the rose. They took sensuous delight in strewing their banquet halls and couches with the petals of Egyptian roses.

Symbol of mysticism: The first simple damask roses, in shades of white and red with but five single petals and a perfume-laden center, were first brought to Europe from Damascus during the Crusades. Later on, in the early days of Christian history, the rose became the holy symbol of the Virgin Mary, the exact antithesis of the earlier pagan idea which symbolized the rose as the blood of the goddess Venus. It was believed that the thorns of the roses pierced the feet of their Goddess of Love as she hastened to the aid of her beloved Adonis.

The Christian symbolism and mysticism of the rose were further perpetuated when the beads of the rosary were molded from the hardened fragrant paste of rose petals. Sometimes, also, the beads were carved from wood to resemble miniature roses. The rose windows of the great cathedrals stand as the eternal symbol of holiness from the time the window became an integral part of early Gothic cathedral architecture. Whoever has stood in silent wonder and admiration opposite the rose window of Chartres; or has gazed across the broad aisles up into the rose window of Saint Stephen of Sens; or has seen the full sunlight streaming through the rose window in The Riverside Church in New York can readily believe that beauty and holiness are inseparable.

The peasants of France in their many distinctive and picturesque villages have set aside a day of celebration each year when the roses are in full bloom. They gaily weave a crown of red roses and present it to a chosen young woman of the village whom they regard as the most virtuous of the younger generation.

We, too, are beginning to have our own traditions. The "Festival of Roses" in Portland, Oregon, the city of roses, has been celebrated so many years in the month of June that it has now become a tradition which other American cities are following. California has its Rose Bowl, and it is quite possible that other states may follow the gay idea.

All the hybrids which we now know have been developed through the centuries from the three original species. Our whole family of roses may be traced back to the CHINA ROSE, *Rosa chinensis,* the ROSE DE PROVINS, *Rosa gallica,* and the DAMASK ROSE, *Rosa damascena.* We owe the beginning of our American hybrids to the Spanish fathers who first brought the damask rose with them to the missions in California.

The hybridization and cultivation of roses is such a highly specialized art that entire volumes are and need to be devoted to them. These paragraphs are included in this volume by virtue of the rose itself. It always has been classed as an herb throughout all its glamorous history.

Uses: The petals of all the varieties of heavily scented roses are the heart and soul of many *sachets, perfumes, flower teas,* and *potpourris.* The culinary uses of the rose petals are probably the most exotic of all the herbs, and their culinary history dates far back into ancient times.

In the early centuries the Persians made a heady wine from the petals of roses, and during the twelfth century in England a rose-petal liqueur was a rare and exotic delicacy.

Today in England the petals of roses are candied, or they are made into jam as they are in India. The native Indians call this rare and delicate condiment "rose-petal preserves" or *Gulkanda.* The word literally means "preserved roses." The exotic delicacy is made from the petals of Malabar roses by a process which has been used in India since early in the fifteenth

century. The fragrant petals are crushed by and placed between the layers of rock candy, then sealed in crocks and set
in the burning hot sun. The rock candy softens and becomes
permeated with and blends into the sweetness and perfume of
the fresh roses. *Gulkanda* is again available in our American
market after an absence of more than twenty years.

England has also kept for us the old Egyptian tradition of
preparing cigarettes with a soft, velvety rose petal at the tip.
These rose-tipped cigarettes may seem a glamorous extravagance, but they are truly a wholly delightful smoking sensa-
tion.

The French attar of roses is perhaps the most fragrant of all
the attars of roses, though India has developed the art of preparing it to a remarkable degree. The skill of the French in
preparing the oil of roses and rose water is world-renowned
and has made France a leader in the preparation of perfumes.
However, rose water and oil of roses are not only valuable
when used to scent perfumes but they also provide extremely
subtle and delicate flavoring in fancy *cakes* and *cookies.*

The French have also developed a *rose petal vinegar* which
is an aged cider vinegar seasoned with herbs and rose petals.
The history of the rose petal vinegar dates back more than 200
years, when it was first brewed in Normandy by an imaginative Frenchwoman whose beautiful rose garden inspired her
to experiment with the uses of rose petals in the culinary art.

Homemakers today who are eager to add the imaginative
touch and a subtle taste to various herb teas will discover that
by blending a few heavily scented dried rose petals with them
an extraordinary flavor and aroma are given to the teas. A
fruit cup or a *fruit salad,* or a *jelly* flavored with the petals of
roses, can be one of the most delightful of taste experiences.
We, too, can rediscover the pleasure of using rose petals with
foods, a delight which the Orientals and many Europeans have
known and enjoyed for centuries.

The Rose

O, how much more doth beauty beauteous seem
By that sweet ornament which truth doth give!
The rose looks fair, but fairer we it deem
For that sweet odor which doth in it live.

The canker-blooms have full as deep a dye
As the perfumed tincture of the roses,
Hang on such thorns and play as wantonly
When summer's breath their masked buds discloses:
But, for their virtue only is their show,
They live unwoo'd and unrespected fade,
Die to themselves. Sweet roses do not so;
Of their sweet deaths are sweetest odors made:
And so of you, beauteous and lovely youth,
When that shall fade, my verse distills your truth.
—WILLIAM SHAKESPEARE

ROSE GERANIUM, *Pelargonium capitalum,* is but one of the many varieties of this handsome tropical perfumed perennial which has found its way into our modern herb gardens.

Sometimes referred to as the *Pelargonium graveolens,* our modern rose geranium has come to us from southern Africa. In the mountains high above Johannesburg the scented geraniums grow wild in their tropical splendor.

It was not until late in the seventeenth century that this fragrant species was known on the Continent. The giant plants were introduced into Algiers, Italy, France, Spain, and England. They were treasured not only for their great beauty but also because of the commercial value of the lasting fragrance of the oil distilled from their foliage. Today perhaps there is no rose geranium fragrance to compare with the English scent of the old-fashioned rose geranium lotion.

Characteristics: The majority of the *pelargoniums* have velvety, deeply cut foliage and take their names from the scent, such as the ROSE-SCENTED, the APPLE-SCENTED, the BALM-SCENTED, and the LEMON-SCENTED. Other popular species are the NUTMEG, ORANGE, PEPPERMINT, and SPICY GERANIUM. The leaves differ in size and markings, depending upon the individual varieties, of which there are too many to include in the chapter of a book. They need a complete book of their own. Their heights also vary from the tiny dwarf species to those which grow more than 4 feet in warm climates and the tropics. Usually the larger the leaves, the more fragrant and spicy they are when gently pressed. The blossoms, too, vary in color and size with the variety. The rose geranium makes a beautiful border plant and grows just as readily as a house plant.

Uses: Not only do the fresh petals add a delicate flavor to various foods and drinks, but they give an undeniably exotic touch to them. More and more our homemakers are discovering that the scented petals of some of our most popular flower-garden plants may be used in foods such as *custards, puddings,* and *cakes.*

The dried petals are included in *herb-tea blends* and in *potpourri mixtures.*

The oil distilled from the foliage has its commercial uses chiefly in *perfumes* and *soaps.*

Cultivating: It is best to propagate this beautiful herb by buying the young plants and setting them about 3 feet apart in the place where they will be left to develop and grow. Choose a very sunny spot where the soil is fairly good and well drained. After the plant is well started, but preferably in the late summer, cuttings may be made. All plants should be taken indoors before there is danger of frost. Also, they may be cut back and stored in the cellar. If watered once a week, they may be replanted out of doors in the early spring.

Harvesting: The leaves may be picked from the stems and dried as are other herbs on a small screen or tray placed in the shade. Store the clean leaves in tightly closed containers ready for use.

ROSEMARY, *Rosmarinus officinalis,* is among the most touchingly romantic of all the herbs. For more than 3,000 years this fragrant, sentimental herb has been used in hundreds of ways for its exceedingly lovely aroma and in myriad symbols of varied significance. The ancient Egyptians and Arabs planted rosemary as a border plant for their luxurious and exotic rose gardens.

There is a legend that the beautiful shade of its soft blue flowers had its beginning during the earliest part of the Christian Era. The wistful saga tells us that the blossoms of pale blue had turned into this incredibly soft and delicate shade of blue after they had been touched by the blue cape of the Virgin Mary as she passed over them on her journeys of compassionate mercy.

Rosemary, like sweet basil and lavender, was always cultivated in the gardens of the many medieval monasteries.

The plant was taken to England by the Romans, as most of England's herbs had been, and rosemary has flourished there ever since. Though it is not an easy plant to grow in most northern climates, the mist of the sea and the dampness of the English climate are what make the herb thrive.

Many a lyric line has been written to tell us of the sweetness of rosemary, symbol of love and remembrance. When we hear the word rosemary we cannot help remembering the sigh of Ophelia as she chants: "There's rosemary, that's for remembrance." Folk songs which have been passed down from one generation to another repeat the symbol in varied language. The wistful lines of a haunting Slovenian folk song are translated to read:

> *Rosemary, how dear to me thou art;*
> *Though thy leaves have fallen one by one,*
> *The pale blue bud he picked for me,*
> *Will bloom forever in my heart.*

English brides, as early as the fifteenth century, wore sprigs of rosemary in their hair and carried the sweet herb in their bridal bouquets. Not only was rosemary used at weddings, but many a funeral decoration for king and commoner was made up of sprays of rosemary. The English still place a wreath of rosemary on the graves of their soldiers on Armistice Day. And the first sprig of rosemary for the passing of George Bernard Shaw came from the garden of Ellen Terry.

Characteristics: Rosemary is an erect perennial evergreen which is somewhat slow in growing but will often reach 5 feet in height. The very narrow leaves are slightly bent as a pine needle is bent and the top side is a bright shiny green, with the underside a downy gray. The herb develops into a shrubby bush and in the warmer climates will make a good hedge. It blossoms during April and May, and the blossoms range from a pale blue to the deeper purplish-blue of its calyx. Its blossoms are attractive to bees.

Uses: The fresh and the dried leaves are unusually pungent and give an exciting flavor to many foods such as *appetizers, eggs, fish, game, meats, poultry, soups,* and *vegetables.*

The dried leaves impart a piny scent to sachets and moth preventives. The oil is used commercially in scenting perfumes and toilet preparations.

Cultivating: Rosemary is usually propagated by cuttings and divisions and its grows readily in a poor, dry, limy soil. It may also be grown from seed, and if so, the seed should be started indoors early in the spring and then transplanted when about an inch high. Place the shrub near the outer edge of the garden where there is plenty of sun and where it will not shade the other plants.

In some European gardens rosemary is planted as a hedge, as it is in Virginia, because the shrub may be clipped as closely as box and hyssop. By the end of the second year the plant will make a dense shrub about 2 feet in diameter, so it is necessary to space the mature plants at least that far apart, if not more. During the winter months in the colder climates, unless the plant is well protected from freezing, it should be brought indoors. The plant generally begins to blossom after it is two years old, though sometimes not until it is somewhat older.

When new cuttings are desired it is quite simple to pull off a sprig of rosemary with the heel attached. Allow the cutting to stand in wet sand until it becomes rooted.

Harvesting: One plant is sufficient for the average family if the plant is grown for culinary purposes only. The leaves may be used as soon as they are grown. Then the pungent taste is warm and a little bitter. The plants may be trimmed back two or three times during the season and the tender leaves and stems placed on a screen to dry in a shady location. The entire dried herb is then crushed and stored in tightly covered containers. If there are any coarse stems they should be picked out, for they have a tendency to be woody.

RUE, *Ruta graveolens,* is surrounded by mysticism, ritual, and legendry throughout all its ancient history. Perhaps no herb can claim as much except the rosemary with which rue is so closely linked in the writings and ceremonies of the ancients.

Like rosemary, rue was one of the herbs grown by Charlemagne, as it was by the monks in the monastery at St. Gall, Switzerland. Today it is commercially cultivated in our Southern and Eastern states and grows wild in beautiful profusion over most of Europe.

Rue has been a symbol of protection from disease since the time of the ancient Greeks, and Romans scattered the fresh herb over the floors of their churches or carried a sprig in their hands to ward off the plague. By the time the cultivation of rue was begun in England early in the thirteenth century, rue had become a symbol of sorrow, regret, and repentance.

The word is still an expressive verb in our vocabulary and reflects the remorse associated with it through the many centuries. Whittier referred most beautifully to its bitterness in those lovely lines: "For one shall grasp and one resign, One drink life's rue, and one its wine."

The stems of rue were used in the early Catholic rituals for sprinkling holy water over the heads of sinners, and through this custom it also became known as the *herb of grace.*

In English fairy tales rue is mentioned as a magic herb capable of keeping the goblins away; but more than that, it was regarded highly as a culinary herb in England. And the Scots always considered rue of primary importance in the herb garden. Therefore, rue is included in this volume since again its culinary use is becoming increasingly more important.

Characteristics: An almost evergreen, woody shrub with tiny, thick, bluish-green leaves about an inch long and ¼ inch wide. Will grow 2 feet high to form a beautiful lacy-looking branching bush suitable for a hedge or border. Thrives best in rather poor soil. Flowers appear the second year during July and resemble a tiny yellow four-leaf clover or star in a green calyx. The fruit or seed is a 4- or 5-lobed capsule containing numerous black seed. Rue readily reseeds and needs to be watched so that it won't spread in unwanted places in the garden.

Uses: The strangely bitter, musty flavor of the freshly minced leaves is being used sparingly but increasingly in many foods such as *cheeses, vegetable-juice cocktails, salads, stews,* and *vegetables.* Industrially the oil of rue is valuable in the preparation of *perfumes.*

Cultivating: Propagation of rue is quite simple as the seed germinate quickly and easily. The herb may also be started from cuttings and root divisions. If you have an experimenting streak in you, the plant makes a most beautiful background and border plant. If sown in poor soil where it is not disturbed, rue will rarely winterkill. Plant the seed in a chalky or lime soil which will receive an average amount of moisture and plenty of sun. Space the mature plants about 18 inches apart, and do not be alarmed if this evergreen turns brown late in the winter. At the first hint of spring the tiny, lacy green leaves will soon be sprouting along the sturdy, bluish stalks.

Harvesting: The herb doesn't blossom until after the second or third year, but since only the tiny leaves are used in cookery, they may be picked early during the first summer.

If desired, the leaves may be dried in the same manner as other herbs and stored for use during the winter months.

SAGE, *Salvia officinalis,* derives its name from the Latin verb *salvare,* to save, and the Latin proverb: *Cur moriatur homo, ciu calvia crescit in horto* [Why should a man die who has sage in his garden]? confirms our knowledge that for centuries sage was highly regarded for its great curative and healing powers. Even today the dried leaves are steeped in boiling water and the sage tea is a favorite spring tonic.

Native to the north Mediterranean countries, sage found its way to Anglo-Saxon England from the monastery gardens of France and Switzerland as early as the fourteenth century. The Saxons used sage not only to flavor pork and other meat dishes, as we do today, but they often cooked the pungent herb with fish. English stuffings and sauces were flavored with sage, especially those stuffings used with geese, veal, and whole roasted pigs.

A delicately colored cheese of seventeenth-century England was called sage cheese, and the modern Dutch, Swiss, and American sage cheeses are sold in our own food shops today.

Characteristics: All the varieties of sage—and there are at least 500 of them—are gray-leaved and shrubby perennials. The different varieties derive their common names from the dominant fragrance of the foliage. For example, the PINE-APPLE SAGE, *Salvia splendens,* which grows 3 feet tall, has the fruity fragrance of pineapple. Its rich-colored red flowers blossom late in the fall. The common name may also indicate the color of the blossoms or the foliage, such as WHITE SAGE, *Salvia officinalis alba,* and the CYPRUS SAGE, which takes its name from its very dark green leaves.

The common sage, *Salvia officinalis,* has light purple blossoms which grow in terminal spikes and are a beautiful sight in the garden. This variety grows about 2 feet tall and makes a lovely appearance in a gray-green garden or as a border for a vegetable garden. Another garden variety, known as *Salvia Horminum,* gives a beautifully vivid purple hue in the garden. This species rarely grows more than 18 inches high.

Still another variety useful and decorative as a back border only, since it grows at least 4 feet tall, is the biennial *Salvia Sclarea,* or CLARY SAGE. Its leaves are more than 8 inches long, and the exquisite blossoms are a pinkish-blue or a pure white. For continuous blossoming, clary sage should be planted each year.

The MEADOW SAGE, *Salvia pratensis,* has the bluest blossoms of all the sages and is most attractive in garden bouquets. The flower buds of the majority of sages, except the pineapple sage, will begin to open in temperate climates about the first or second week in May and continue blossoming through June and July. Bees are attracted to all the varieties.

Sage will grow in practically any climate in the world, from the coolness of Maine and northern Europe down through the temperate and warmer zones on both continents. The soil should be sandy and well drained, and the plant needs full sunshine.

Uses: Sage is one of the most important herbs for seasoning foods. Both the dried and the fresh whole leaves are universally used; and the powdered, dried sage is an absolute necessity in the preparation of many prepared meats and sausages. America cannot cultivate enough sage for home consumption and annually imports thousands of tons of DALMATIAN SAGE, which grows wild on the rocky hills of Serbia (Yugoslavia). Homemakers use this marvelously aromatic herb in many foods such as *appetizers, cheeses, fish, shellfish, game, meats, poultry, soups, sauces, stuffings,* and *stews.*

Cultivating: The two popular culinary species are the common garden sage, *Salvia officinalis,* and the white sage, *Salvia officinalis alba.* Like all the sages, the seed of these fragrant varieties germinate easily and will thrive in a fairly good soil which is well drained. Sage may be started from seed sown either in the spring or the autumn, and the plants are easily increased by cuttings. Fall cuttings may be set in sand and placed in a cold frame through the winter months, then transplanted in the spring after they are well rooted.

If seed are sown early in the spring, the seedlings should be thinned when they are about 2 or 3 inches high. The mature plants of the common garden sages should stand from 12 to 18 inches apart in rows that are separated at least 3 feet. The larger varieties, such as the pineapple and the clary sage, naturally need more space and should stand at least 2 feet apart in rows that are separated 3 feet.

Well-developed sage plants need only a light protection of leaves during the winter weather. They should be pruned in the early spring just as the new leaves begin to make their appearance. All the dead woody twigs should be cut away, especially the central stem.

For the average family two or three plants will be sufficient, since sage increases so rapidly. And even though the plants have a tendency to become woody, with care they should last 4 or 5 years. Many gardeners, however, renew their sage beds every 3 years by burning down the old plants and allowing the ashes to nourish the ground.

Harvesting: The best-quality leaves are those from the tender young shoots cut near the top of the plant before it blossoms. During the first season these stems may be cut off 3 inches from the top as soon as the plant has grown about 8 inches tall. Fresh leaves may also be picked by hand for use from time to time during the entire season. If the plants are well established, they may be cut two or three times during the first season; but only one picking is always safe.

After the first season, two or three pickings and cuttings may be made regularly during the season. Dry the cuttings quickly by tying them in a clean white cloth bag hung over the heat of a stove. The leaves will then retain their natural color and flavor. Whole leaves may be carefully removed from stems and packed in tightly corked bottles for use as needed. For powdered sage, leaves may be pulverized as soon as dried, or stored whole and pulverized when used.

SAVORY or **SUMMER SAVORY,** *Satureia hortensis,* is another herb native to Europe's Mediterranean countries which has become a great favorite in the herb gardens of the world.

Several species of the savories were used by the Greeks and Romans for centuries, and they often blended a savory with wild thyme to flavor their soups, stuffings, meats, and game. Like so many of the herbs which the Romans took to England with them, savory became extremely popular and soon found an important place in Saxon recipes. Summer savory was one of the herbs of the famous garden of the Monastery of St. Gall, and Charlemagne also grew the savories in his gardens.

From England the colonists eventually brought the herb to America, and it has remained one of our favorite seasonings.

At one time the principal source of supply for the American market was from southern France. Since the flavor of the *Satureia hortensis* is best when the herb is picked in the early summer, it became known by the common name of SUM-

MER SAVORY. The WINTER SAVORY, *Satureia montana,* is a sturdier herb and grows here as a perennial.

Characteristics: Savory or summer savory. Fragrant annual with slender woody stems, grows 18 inches high but has a tendency to spread and fall over, which gives it a bushy appearance. In Switzerland and other parts of Europe summer savory is commonly called *Bohnenkraut,* which means "the herb of the string bean." Today summer savory adds flavor not only to the string bean but to many other green vegetables to which a few of its aromatic leaves have been added in the process of cooking.

The leaves are small, ½ inch long, narrow, blunt-tipped, dark green, and the entire plant is covered with tiny pink flowers similar to other herbs of the mint, *Labiatae,* family to which it belongs. Twenty to thirty plants are more than enough for average family use.

Characteristics: Savory or winter savory. This is a smaller plant than the summer savory and seldom grows more than 15 inches high. Its stems are slender and weak, but since the plants self-sow so easily, winter savory makes a colorful and beautiful border plant along the edges of an herb or rock garden. It is one of the herbs which edges the Mount Vernon Herb Garden.

The flowers of the winter savory are usually a deeper hue than those of the summer savory but may range in color from a pinkish-white to a warm purple. Its shiny leaves have a stronger aroma than those of summer savory, but both the dried and the fresh leaves are used as seasoning as those of the summer savory are.

Uses: The piquant flavor of both the savories makes these herbs unusually useful in giving a more delicious flavor to many foods such as *eggs, fish, game, meats, poultry, salads, sauces, soups,* and *green vegetables.* Two or three leaves of savory placed in the water in which turnips or cabbage are poached will practically eliminate the strong, natural aroma of these vegetables.

Cultivating: Summer savory. The seed of the summer savory may be sown early in the spring as soon as all danger of frost is past. A dry, gravelly, moderately rich soil where there is plenty of sun is the best for this herb. The seed should be sown in shallow drills of ½ inch in rows about 12 inches apart. The mature plants should be spaced about 6 inches; and since they grow very quickly, they may be planted at regular intervals of

3 weeks if a large quantity of the herb is desired. Keep well weeded.

Winter savory. Seed may be sown in the early spring in a rather poor soil that is well drained and where there is full sunshine. The herb may also be propagated from cuttings of the new growth, and since the woody stalks of the herb spread rapidly over the ground, it is best to set the cuttings at least 2 feet apart to give the plant plenty of room. To induce a full, heavy growth of new leaves, the shrub should be kept fairly well clipped. Winter savory will winterkill if the soil is rich and damp. As with many herbs, a poor, light soil gives the best results.

Harvesting: Summer savory. Some of the tender young tips may be cut any time during the season. By midsummer, when the herb begins to blossom, the whole plant may be pulled up ready for drying, or only from 6 to 8 inches of the top growth may be cut. The stems may be tied in small bunches and hung up to dry, or spread on clean screens in a shady, airy spot until thoroughly dried. Strip the leaves from the stems and remove all small pieces of woody stems so that only the leaves are stored. Place them in small tightly covered containers. Use whole leaves or crushed, as desired.

Harvesting: Winter savory. The tender young tips and leaves may be used fresh or dried as one uses summer savory or thyme. For winter use cut only the tenderest tips and flowering tops at the very beginning of the flowering season. The herb may be hung in small bunches or spread on a screen in a shady, dry spot. When the leaves are dry, remove from the stems and store them in a tightly closed container until needed.

SESAME SEED, *Sesamum orientale,* is the seed or dried fruit of a strong, tall, beautiful annual which, when growing in a large field, bends and sways in the wind like wheat.

China, India, and Turkey cultivate this sturdy, straight plant with its long, tapering dark green leaves which are soft and fuzzy. The square stems of the *Sesamum orientale* grow from 1 to 2 feet high, and the blossoms grow close to the stem. The lovely tubular flowers about an inch long resemble the foxglove, and they vary in color from a creamy white to a deep lavender. The seed pod forms within the blossom.

The sesame seed were known to the ancient Greeks and Hebrews, and for centuries the Egyptian and Persian tribes used the ground seed as a food grain as we use rye for rye bread. The Romans used both the cumin and the sesame seed, when crushed into a paste, as a spread over bread as we use butter.

Practically every child is familiar with the magic phrase from *Ali Baba and the Forty Thieves* as Ali Baba hears the robbers' chieftain command the cave to "Open sesame" or "Close sesame." But history has mentioned the sesame plant centuries before the tale in the *Arabian Nights* was even thought of. The plant was growing in the rich, verdant valley of the river Nile long before the time of Moses.

However, the exact origin of the *Sesamum orientale* is lost in history, but present-day botanists tell us that the sesame seed may just as easily have originated in Africa rather than in Asia. Whether from Asia or from Africa, this most valuable and delectable nutty-flavored seed is being cultivated for greater commercial purposes in many countries of the world. Mr. J. A. Martin, associate horticulturist of the South Carolina Experiment Station in Clemson, is carrying on extensive plant-breeding experiments with this herb, which he identifies as the *Sesamum indicum.* He hopes to develop a new non-shattering type of sesame which will combine all the desirable qualities of the plant, including high yield and resistance to disease. He reports that sesame seed from Australia, Burma, China, Colombia, Guatemala, Hawaii, India, Korea, Mexico, Nicaragua, Russia, South Africa, and Turkey are being used in the work of the various experimental stations in the plan to develop a type of sesame in which the mature seed will not drop prior to the harvesting of it. Other experimental stations in the Rio Grande Valley of Texas and throughout the cotton belt are being supplied with seed through the research work being carried on under Mr. Martin's supervision.

Characteristics: The sesame plant is most decorative in gardens situated in regions where there is a long, warm summer. The variety grown in America has much the same physical characteristics as the oriental variety described in a previous paragraph. Grown for its seed, which when hulled is oval and pointed at one end. Creamy white in color, it is rarely more than ⅛ inch in length.

Uses: Sesame seed, whole or crushed, is a staple food in India and the Orient. The rich, nutty flavor of the whole seed is highly valued in America for its use in preparing baked goods and confectionery, especially *Halvah.* The seed also add a nutlike richness to such foods as *cakes, cookies, cheeses, salads, soups,* and *vegetables.* Industrially the sesame seed are valuable for the oil used in the manufacture of *oleomargarine, cosmetics,* and *soap.*

Cultivating: Early in the spring the seed may be sown in a hotbed and the seedlings transplanted to another hotbed until they have been well established and strong. Select a sunny spot where the soil is rich and well drained. Transplant again about 8 inches apart and keep the plants free from weeds at all times. With a long, warm, constant temperature, the plants will grow rapidly and mature within 90 to 120 days. The buds mature so quickly that it is said that one can stand by and actually watch them open.

Harvesting: The seed does not mature in the northern climates. However, where the summers are long and warm, the seed pods should be cut from the stems before they are so dry that they will shatter. (This holds true, of course, until the perfect non-shattering type of sesame will be readily obtainable.) Spread the sesame pods on a clean tray in a dry, airy, shady spot. When thoroughly dry, the seed will fall from the pods and all chaff should be blown away. Continue to dry the seed until all signs of moisture have disappeared. Then store the perfectly dry seed in tightly closed containers until ready for use.

SHALLOT, *Allium ascalonicum,* is one of the important garden herbs which is not really a true species. No wild shallots have ever been found; however like the onion whose history is lost in antiquity, the botanists believe that the shallot came from Syria and that it was there that it had been developed as one of the varieties of the true onion, *Allium cepa.*

Near the shores of Lake Constance in northeastern Switzerland, the shallot was grown in the gardens of the Monastery of St. Gall as early as the ninth century. By the sixteenth century England was cultivating these small, flavorsome bulbs. Since they were always used sparingly as garlic, the misleading name of SPANISH GARLIC was given them.

Today the shallot is cultivated chiefly in our Southern states, particularly in Louisiana, and often is called the Louisiana shallot. See also Chives, Garlic, Leek, and Onion.

Characteristics: The plant has slender awl-shaped leaves and the root forms clusters or clumps of small grayish bulbs which are sometimes referred to as cloves of shallot. When dried, the tiny round bulbs from ½ to ¾ inch in diameter turn a deep pink or reddish-brown. The flavor is much more delicate than that of any of the onion family.

Uses: The ways in which the individual and distinctive flavor of the shallot may be used are as varied as the many uses of the onion. The shallot gives the epicurean touch to much of European cookery and imparts a subtle deliciousness to such foods as *fish, game, meats, poultry, sauces,* and *stuffings.*

Cultivating: Under certain very favorable conditions the shallot plants will blossom and produce seed, but the herb is practically always propagated by planting the new shoots or small divisions that develop in the clump of plants. The division or clove of the shallot is planted like garlic cloves in a moderately rich, sandy soil which has plenty of moisture and is kept well drained. In the Southern states the shallot divisions are usually planted in the autumn for a winter crop; however, very early spring planting has proved equally successful.

Harvesting: When the tops begin to wilt and turn yellow the bulb is ready to be pulled from the earth. The entire plant (the bulb with the foliage) is dried in the open air for at least 2 days. Then the tops are cut off and the small bulbs are stored in baskets or porous sacks placed in a cool, dry place where no frost can reach them. When properly stored in this manner, the bulbs will keep perfectly for an entire year.

SORREL or **GARDEN SORREL,** *Rumex acetosa,* with a history that dates back more than 3,000 years B.C., is still found growing wild in the meadows of Asia, Europe, and many parts of North America.

The Egyptians learned that the sharp, sour flavor of the sorrel was a perfect combination with other greens. The Romans, too, were partial to the distinctive taste, and when the raw sorrel leaves were combined with lettuce the combination was served preceding a heavy banquet so that the rich foods which followed might be enjoyed.

It took more than 4,000 years for this lowly herb of the fields to become known as a culinary favorite in England. Early in the thirteenth century sorrel was listed as an English herb for use in sauces, and by the sixteenth century the English had learned to excel in the making of *sorrel soup.* In some parts of

England today the tart soup is still served. A *sorrel sauce* is prepared and served with roast beef, mutton, and even poultry.

Our own colonists planted sorrel in Salem and used the first tender green leaves of the early springtime as a salad green as well as a cooked vegetable.

Characteristics: Hardy perennial which flourishes in a rich, moist soil in the full sunshine in warm and temperate climates. The herb is often called SOUR GRASS since the flavor of the long, pinnate leaves is sharp and acid. It reaches a height of at least 3 feet.

FRENCH SORREL, *Rumex scutatus,* has a broader leaf than the species known as the garden sorrel, and though its branches fall over, it may reach a height of 2 feet. The round, green-colored flower heads of the French and the garden sorrel grow at the top of tall spikes. The MOUNTAIN SORREL, *Oxyria digyna,* which grows wild in the Alps, has flowers of a deep purple shade.

The variety of sorrel most popular in many of the American herb gardens is called the SILVER LEAF.

Uses: The fresh young tender green leaves may be used in combination *green salads* or cooked in combination with other greens such as *cabbage, lettuce, beet tops,* or *spinach.*

Cultivating: Sorrel is easily grown from seed and the planting should take place in early spring in a moist soil where there is plenty of sunshine. The plant increases rapidly through its creeping roots and can easily become a pest. To prevent this, it should be dug up, the roots divided, and then replanted at least once every 4 years. The mature plants should be spaced from 1½ to 2 feet apart, and six plants will produce enough leaves for the average family's use.

Harvesting: The young tender leaves appear in the garden even before all the snow has gone, and these green shoots may be used as soon as they push their way through. During the first of the season the leaves are picked and used the same as garden spinach. But by the time the stalks are filled with blossoms the leaves have become too tough and bitter for use.

TANSY or **FERN-LEAVED TANSY,** *Tanacetum vulgare,* var. *crispum,* again is fast becoming a great favorite in both herb and flower gardens because of its rich green color, decorative foliage, and vivid flower buttons.

The word "tansy" comes from the Greek word meaning "immortality." Since some of the plants retain so much of their natural color and the golden yellow of the flower heads remains golden even when dried, it is easily understood how the herb was christened with such a name.

Tansy grew in the herb gardens of Charlemagne and was cultivated by the Benedictine monks of St. Gall. And at one time during early English history mention is made of tansy cakes, puddings, and tea. All of these were served in the beginning of the springtime because they were believed to be good for one's health.

During the months of July, August, and September the wild tansy blossoms in profusion along the roadsides in our New England and Southern states. In the Middle West, especially in Michigan and Indiana, there is a revival of its commercial cultivation; and culinary experts again are beginning to use this bitter herb for its piquancy in flavoring certain foods.

Those who venture with new and exciting flavors in foods may well take courage, since no less an epicurean authority on fish than Izaak Walton has written for us to heed his recommendation of "excellent Minnow-Tansies; being fried with yolks of eggs, the flowering cowslips, and of primrose, and a little tansy; thus make a dainty dish." The Sicilians today are masters in the art of preparing *fritelle di pesciolini,* "minnow pancakes," a delicate fish dish prepared with the tiniest of shining silver minnows or sardines.

Characteristics: The fern-leaved tansy with its beautiful dark green foliage has finely divided fernlike leaves which branch out from the stout, reddish, smooth, erect stems which grow from 2½ to 3 feet tall. Each leaf is about 6 inches long with saw-toothed edges divided almost to the center. This gives the leaf its lacy, ferny appearance. The golden-yellow, hard, buttonlike flowers, produced in clusters at the top, blossom for about 3 months in midsummer, usually from July through September. Beautiful as a back flower border.

The COMMON TANSY, *Tanacetum vulgare,* which grows wild along the roadsides, is less delicate-looking and grows almost 4 feet high. Its sturdy stalks make a very unusual hedge if the plant is kept from going to seed by cutting off the flower heads as they appear.

Uses: The leafy tips of both varieties of tansy have medicinal and industrial value, especially in the preparation of *cosmetics,* *toilet waters, ointments,* and in the *liqueur* Chartreuse. Its culinary uses are beginning to come into their own again, and the fresh, tender young leaves may be sparingly used to add a new interest to an *omelet,* a *baked fish,* or a *meat pie.* A *tansy tea,* brewed from either the fresh or dried crushed leaves, is said to have a valuable calming effect upon the nerves.

Cultivating: Tansy may be grown from seed in almost any good, fairly moist soil which is well drained. If an early spring start is desired, the seed may be planted during the last weeks of autumn before the first frost. The seed will not germinate during the late fall. It is also an easy herb to propagate by root division in the early spring. The rows should be at least 3 feet apart and the plants spaced at 18 inches to allow plenty of room for the sturdy stems. The herb grows easily and has a tendency to spread. If it spreads too much, pieces of the root should be dug out to prevent the herb from getting out of bounds.

Harvesting: The tender young leaves may be picked and used as needed. If the plant is cultivated for commercial purposes, it is cut from its stem late in the summer, when it is in full bloom. The leaves and tops are separated from the stems. The leaves are carefully dried on screens in the shade so they will retain their natural color, but the stems are left lying in the field until all the moisture has evaporated. The leaves are stored in tightly closed containers.

To dry tansy buttons for winter bouquets, cut flowers only when freshly opened. Tie in small loose bunches and hang in cool, shady, airy place to dry. Arrange in bouquets as desired.

TARRAGON or **FRENCH TARRAGON,** *Artemisia dracunculus,* was one of the favorite herbs in the gardens of Charlemagne and remained a favorite with epicures through all its long years of history.

Centuries before Charlemagne the Greeks and Egyptians cultivated the astringent, aromatic tarragon and developed it to a degree that made it one of the most cherished of herbs. The English grew fond of its almost spicy taste, and the French discovered that tarragon vinegar, their now famous *vinaigre d'estragon,* was a gourmet's specialty. To this day the epicure treasures *tarragon vinegar* as one of the most important ingredients of a particularly delicious salad dressing.

Characteristics: The true French tarragon is a bushy, hardy perennial in New England. In France the herb is grown as an annual. In the United States, as a vigorous perennial, tarragon is adaptable to various growing conditions. The plants rarely form seed but are easily propagated by root or crown divisions. The narrow dark green leaves about an inch long and ⅛ inch wide are spaced at irregular intervals on woody stems. The plant grows from 18 inches to 2 feet tall but has a tendency to spread close to the ground. When it blossoms, the flowers are inconspicuous little clusters of yellowish or pinkish-white.

Uses: Both the fresh young leaves and the dried tarragon are a highly valued and delicious seasoning in such foods as *appetizers, eggs, fish, shellfish, meats, poultry, salads, soups, sauces,* and *vinegar.* The dried leafy tips are valuable industrially in perfumes, toilet waters, and confectionery.

Cultivating: Tarragon thrives practically anywhere in the garden, in the sun or in the partial shade where the soil is well drained. Since it does not develop fertile seed in America, tarragon must be grown from root divisions or cuttings, or small plants readily purchased from a nursery may be set out. In the colder climates these young plants should not be transplanted after the middle of June, for there will not be sufficient time for them to become well enough established to withstand the winter. Protect plants with a leaf mulch during the coldest months.

Root divisions should be made early in the spring when the perennial is not more than 2 inches high. Lift the whole plant carefully in order not to break the tender roots. Leave 2 shoots on each root. Set the root divisions at intervals of about 18 inches in rows at least 3 feet apart.

If propagated from cuttings of the older plants, cut at least 4 inches long and allow them to develop roots in moist, clean sand. Cuttings should be set out no later than August.

The rapidly entangling shallow roots of the tarragon should be dug up and the roots subdivided and transplanted at least once every 3 years. In milder climates this may be done at practically any time during the year. Otherwise, never transplant after August.

Harvesting: As soon as the tiny plants have become well established, the tender leaves and tops may be used fresh as needed. If the plant is cut back several times during the summer season, this will encourage new tender young growths.

When the herb is to be dried for winter use at any time during the season, the young leaves and tops should be placed on a tray or a fine clean screen in a shady, airy place. As soon as well dried, the leaves should be placed in tightly covered containers for use as needed.

THYME, *Thymus vulgaris,* is among the most highly favored of herbs for its varied species of great beauty and for its more than usual usefulness to mankind.

Centuries ago the Greeks used sprigs of thyme as sweet-burning incense in the temples long before it became popular as a culinary herb. The floors of banquet halls, churches, and monasteries were strewn with thyme, and it was planted on the graves of heroes. Greek poets and scholars wrote of the delightful perfume of thyme as they did of other aromatic herbs; and Kipling compared the odor to the perfume of the "dawn in Paradise."

In medieval history mention is also made of *thyme honey,* which today is coming back into our markets from abroad. The thyme honey of Sicily has a flavor all its own and has been highly prized for hundreds of years. All along the eastern coast of Italy herds of sheep are sent to graze over the fields of thyme. Feeding on the sweetness of the herb gives to the lamb and mutton from this section a most delightful and individual flavor.

Early in the twelfth century thyme had become a favorite culinary herb in England; and Izaak Walton mentions thyme as a necessary and delectable seasoning for all fish.

Characteristics: Among the more than 60 varieties of thyme, there are several beautiful members of the species which can be grown and are widely cultivated in Canada and the United States, as well as in the countries nearer its native Mediterranean and Asia Minor regions.

Thyme is a bushy perennial which makes a most attractive border in the garden. If planted for culinary use only, a dozen plants will be more than ample for the average family.

The trailing varieties of thyme that are most beautiful and useful in rock gardens are the *Thymus serpyllum cocineus,* with brilliant scarlet blossoms, and the *Thymus serpyllum albus,* with its snowy white. The WOOLLY THYME, *Thymus serpyllum lanuginosus,* with its lavender blossoms, spreads or trails decumbent along the earth; and the WILD THYME, *Thymus serpyllum*, will spread rapidly in any garden.

Among the culinary varieties is the well-loved broad-leaved ENGLISH or GARDEN THYME, *Thymus vulgaris*. It grows about a foot tall and is one of the loveliest of the gray-green plants of the garden. Its foliage is almost evergreen, and the pale lavender or purple blossoms attract the bees all during the month of June.

LEMON THYME, *Thymus serpyllum*, var. *citriodorus*, is one of the trailing varieties which is also a culinary favorite. This lovely herb with its pink blossoms and golden-green leaves presents a beautiful sight during the month of July, when it is in full bloom.

Uses: The strong, pungent flavor of thyme can be one of the most subtle of seasoning herbs when used with real restraint and culinary artfulness. The tender young leaves, either dried or fresh, are used to season many foods such as *sea-food cocktails,* in *herb bouquets,* in *cheeses.* Also in *fish* and *sea-food chowders, eggs, game, shellfish, meats, poultry, salads, sauces, soups, stuffings,* and *vegetables.*

The dried flowers are wonderfully sweet in *sachets* and *pot-pourris* and add delicious flavor to blends of *herb teas.*

Cultivating: Thyme is best propagated from seed sown indoors or under glass in an outdoor bed. When 2 or 3 inches high the young plants are set from 10 to 18 inches apart in rows separated 3 feet. (The low spreading varieties are set 18 inches apart and the more erect plants about 10 inches apart.) The seed are so tiny that it is best to mix them with sand before planting. This is best accomplished by simply pressing them lightly into the earth. Thyme requires very little care. However, it requires plenty of sun and the soil should be well drained, dry, and rather sandy. To prevent the herb from becoming woody, it is best to renew the planting every 2 years.

Harvesting: Leaves. Several inches of the tender tips and stems may be cut either just before the herb blossoms or while it is in full bloom. A few tiny fresh leaves may be picked as desired for use fresh from time to time. The herb usually begins to blossom early in June and continues in full bloom for many weeks. To dry the herb, tie the cut stems into loose bundles. Hang them in a shady, airy spot. When dry, the leaves may be stripped by hand and stored in tightly covered containers. Also, it is possible to store the dried stems and leaves in large bags.

Flowers. The flowers may also be gathered separately if desired. If so, they should be placed on a fine screen in a shady, airy spot. When dried, the flowers may be stored separately for use in *sachets, teas,* and *potpourris.*

VERBENA or **LEMON VERBENA,** *Lippia citriodora,* though often referred to as an "old-fashioned herb," is really quite young and new in American gardens.

The species of lemon-scented verbena with which we are so familiar did not reach us until early in the eighteenth century. It was only then that it was brought to America as one of the beautiful wild flowers of South America. For centuries previously the Spaniards had used the delicately scented lemon-verbena leaves in brewing herb teas, and they still use the tea as a great liquid delicacy.

The botanical *Verbena officinalis,* or vervain, which is the "verbena of Europe" and a related genus, is not to be confused in history with our much more recently developed lemon verbena. The vervain has been mentioned in history countless times and was evidently one of Virgil's favorites. He wrote often of this aromatic herb and invariably spoke of it as "holy" and "rich." It was this verbena which was among the sacred herbs of Greece and not our lemon verbena.

The vervain native to the United States is the *Verbena hastata,* a tall, handsome perennial with a four-angled stem which grows 3 or 4 feet tall. The leaves are serrate, acuminate, petiolate, and hastate. The flower is a small, purplish-blue sessile one which is arranged on tall spikes. This vervain, sometimes called WILD HYSSOP, grows along roadsides and in dry grassy fields and blossoms all summer from June to September. In England this vervain usually blossoms in the month of July only and then goes to seed. Its uses are entirely medicinal and the herb is said to be helpful in reducing coughs.

Characteristics: Lemon verbena is a tender herb, delicately scented and graceful-looking. It thrives best in warm and moderately warm temperatures. The narrow lemon-scented yellowish-green leaves are pointed at the tips and grow along woody but graceful stems in whorls of 3 or 4. The aromatic leaves are charmingly decorative in flower arrangements. The flowers vary in shades of pale blue to pinkish-lavender and are quite inconspicuous even though they grow in slender spikes.

Uses: The leaves are valuable industrially chiefly for their use in the manufacture of *toilet waters* and *perfumes*. Their culinary uses add beauty and an exotic touch to such foods as *fruit salads* and *iced beverages*. Homemakers, alert to the fragrance of the lemon-verbena leaves, are beginning to use them as flavoring in *jellies, custards,* and *appetizers*. When the leaves are placed in *sachets* their fragrance will be strong and pronounced for about 6 months. Then suddenly the fragrance fades away and the leaves lose all their aromatic value.

Cultivating: Lemon verbena needs a moderately rich soil, well drained, and a place in the garden where there is full sunshine. The herb is usually propagated from cuttings though seed are available. The slips or cuttings should be at least 3 or 4 inches long and may be rooted easily by placing them in wet sand and keeping them warm. At least 55° F. to 60° F. is best.

The mature plants should be set about 2 feet apart, depending upon the locality in which the verbena is growing. In very warm climates it may grow as high as 10 feet, but the average height in the more temperate climates is about 3 feet.

When grown as a house plant lemon verbena rarely reaches more than 10 inches in height. In the early fall, in cold climates, the plants may be brought indoors, or they may be cut back and stored in a cool dark place where the temperature will not fall below 55° F. Very early in the spring the weak stalks should be cut off and the plants repotted in new soil. The new green growth of fragrant leaves will grow along the woody dead-looking stems and soon be ready again for use as cuttings.

Harvesting: The fresh tender leaves may be picked from the stems all during the summer months, and during the winter also when taken indoors. To have dried leaves for sachets and teas, they should be picked in the early fall, placed on screens or trays in a dry, airy spot. When completely dried, the leaves may be stored in tightly closed containers until ready for use.

WATER CRESS, *Sisymbrium nasturtium aquaticum,* is native to the temperate zones of Europe but was taken to Africa, England, and America to be cultivated, as were so many of the herbs of the ancients. See also Cress or Land Cress.

The cresses, both land and water, were known to the ancient Egyptians, Greeks, Persians, and Romans. The latter used water cress as a favorite pre-banquet salad, and it is still popular as such with the modern Greeks. More and more, Americans are using this tasty little herb in combination with other greens, both cooked and raw, as well as in the English manner of cooking it in soups and as a vegetable.

Early in the ninth century water cress was among the herbs grown in the gardens of the monastery in St. Gall, Switzerland. Though essentially a water plant, cress thrives in a rich, moist, limy soil almost as well. After centuries the plant found its way into England and English cookery. From there it reached America, where it continues to increase in commercial and culinary importance.

Characteristics: A peppery little perennial which grows from 5 to 6 inches high in clear, running brooks and streams in all the temperate zones throughout the world. Today it is found wild practically all over the United States and is grown commercially in our Southern and Western states, especially Alabama, California, and Virginia. The dark green glossy leaves are almost round and grow on paler green stems. The tiny 4-petaled white flowers blossom in clusters practically all summer long. The pungent flavor is very similar to that of the nasturtium.

Uses: The tender young fresh leaves add attractiveness to many foods as a *garnish*. As a flavoring, the chopped leaves are blended with such foods as *appetizers, biscuits* and *breads, cheeses, eggs, fish, shellfish, meats, pastries, salads, sandwiches,* and *soups*. As a vegetable, water cress may be blended with other greens and cooked as one cooks spinach or dandelion greens.

Cultivating: Water cress, as its name implies, thrives best in shallow, clear brooks and ponds where there is plenty of lime. If there is no running brook nearby, one may be improvised if the plants are set in long, narrow ditches or trenches protected by a framework of boards. As the plant grows, running water is gradually allowed to flow in until it almost covers the little plants which are about 5 inches tall. However, the plants may also be set in any rich, very moist soil to which lime has been added. The stems root very easily at the nodes when placed in water; and if lime is added to this water, it improves the results. A new bed may be started while another is being used for cuttings, and it is best to renew the beds frequently.

Harvesting: The young, tender leaves and stems are cut continuously after about 30 days. As long as the weather is mild enough, the plant keeps right on growing and the harvest can be a constant one.

WOODRUFF or **SWEET WOODRUFF**, *Asperula odorata*, is often called by its Teutonic common name, WALDMEISTER, or MASTER OF THE WOODS. It is found growing wild in all the sheltered forests of Europe and southern Asia, especially along the river Rhine and in the Black Forest of Germany. There, as in other shady forests, this lovely herb covers the ground with its blanket of deep green leaves and clusters of 4-petaled flowers which look like tiny stars scattered loosely through the thickly whorled stems.

Because of its penetrating sweetness, woodruff was used as a strewing herb for centuries. As the beautiful foliage was crushed by the feet of those who walked over it, the strong fragrance was released and filled the air with its perfume.

As early as the thirteenth century woodruff became popular in Germany, England, and Sweden as a flavoring herb for wines and liqueurs. Its fragrant sweetness is still in use today, and *May wine* is always flavored with woodruff.

In the English gardens of the fifteenth century woodruff was cultivated for its decorative use in garlands and bouquets. We are told that when the herb is in full bloom in June there are those in England who still carry a spray of fragrant woodruff as they go to church on St. Barnabas Day, just as they did centuries ago.

Characteristics: A spreading, creeping perennial about 12 inches tall which clings close to the ground and makes a luxuriant, matlike carpet of deep green. Woodruff thrives in complete shade or in a partially shady spot, and the soil should be loose, moist, sandy loam, well drained. Will grow in practically all temperate and moderately warm zones. The herb usually blossoms during May, June, and July. Woodruff is lovely in a rock garden if controlled and not allowed to spread too much. The starry flowers are uncommonly attractive in bouquets.

Uses: The leaves of sweet woodruff have industrial value especially in the manufacture of *sachets*, fancy *snuffs*, *wines*, and *liqueurs*. Both the fresh and the dried leaves may be used to add a new fragrance to *herb teas*, as well as flavor to cooling *fruit beverages* and *wines*. The small sprigs of the flowering tips of woodruff are also used as *garnishes* for many summer beverages.

Cultivating: The seed of the woodruff germinate so slowly that it is best to propagate the herb by root divisions. These are readily obtainable from nurseries and herb gardens. The root divisions should be set about 12 inches apart, and if a thick carpet is the aim when planting woodruff, the herb should not be disturbed.

If cuttings are taken from the mature plants, they may be set in wet sand to take root either in the fall or very early spring. They will root in about 3 weeks and are easy to propagate.

Harvesting: Fresh sprigs and tender leaves may be picked before the plant blossoms when one wishes to use the fresh herb. To dry for winter uses, the stems and flowers may be cut and placed on a tray or screen in a shady, airy place. When thoroughly dried, the leaves and flowers should be stripped from the stems by hand and stored in tightly closed containers. The dried flowers and leaves have an aroma like the sweetness of alfalfa as it lies drying in the warm autumn sun.

CHAPTER EIGHT

Spices
and Caravans

The Arabs were the first traders to bring many of the precious Far Eastern spices to the market places of the Roman world. With soft, silent tread the cushioned camel caravans wove their slow and treacherous journeys across the desert sands to reach the wealthy city of Venice. The wily Arabs refused to answer truthfully the questioning Romans who bought of their wares and who marveled at the delicious scent of the reddish-brown cinnamon quills. They prized the cinnamon aroma so highly that they were willing and eager to go in search of it themselves.

The shrewd and cunning traders refused to reveal the true source of cinnamon and invented fantastic stories when the Romans tried to find out where the delightfully aromatic cinnamon bark could be found. The Arabs told them that no one had ever seen a cinnamon tree but that they had discovered a place where strange and ferocious birds had built nests made from the branches of the cinnamon. To secure the branches, they related, the dangerous birds had to be lured from their nests. This the traders declared they did by offer-

143

ing the huge birds tremendous pieces of raw meat. The birds carried the meat back to the nests, and the weight of the meat caused the nests to fall apart. Then the traders gathered the branches from the ground at the risk of life itself.

By inventing such tales the Arabs could keep the price of the spice as high as a king's ransom. And when one story grew stale they invented another. They finally admitted that they had seen the cinnamon trees but that the trees grew in the center of a mysterious lake which was guarded by griffin vultures. The moment anyone attempted to steal the branches of the fragrant, bushy trees the vultures swooped down to attack the thieves.

For centuries on end the Arab traders kept the prices of spices so high that only kings and monarchs could afford to use them. But the Romans introduced spices to Europe, and as knowledge of them became more general, rulers of the world vied with each other for the control of the spice trade. As commerce grew and transportation became less hazardous, new trade routes were established through exploration expeditions sponsored by kings and queens. Empires were built with the moneys made by trading in spices. (In the twelfth century cloves cost more than $20 a pound.)

England formed a "Guild of Pepperers" in A.D. 1180. Other nations also established monopolies on certain spices in the attempt to control prices. During this time, and all through the Middle Ages, a Mohammedan Federation had complete control of all the caravan routes across the Arabian Desert and of all the transportation from the Near East to the Orient by way of the Red Sea. This control was one of the chief reasons that inspired Columbus to search for a new, shorter route to the Netherlands East Indies and the Malay Peninsula. We, and all in the spice trade, owe much to Columbus. His accidental discovery of our continent led to our subsequent trade with China, the East Indies, and India, and to our development as a world power.

Today the one major spice which reaches us from the British West Indies is allspice, but most of our spices come to us from the East Indies. Great quantities are imported from China, Japan, the Malay Peninsula, the Molucca Islands (so often referred to as the Spice Islands), Java, Borneo, Sumatra, and Bali. India supplies most of the world with mace, pepper, and saffron, as well as huge quantities of ginger. See also chapters devoted to each spice.

ELEPHANT BELLS AND PATIMARS

The sound of the soft tread of the spice-laden camel cara-vans is gone, but the varied, high and thin, or low and rich tones of the elephant bells still respond to the measured step of the East Indian elephants laden with bales of spice being brought to the warehouses for export. The rhythmic swish of the soft paddles of the *patimars* (native boats) in the rivers and waterways of India is a daily occurrence. The natives, in their cradlelike boats, transport the bales of spices from the plantations to the seaports along the coast. From the *patimars* the bales are often transferred to tenders and then to the holds of the freighters waiting to take the precious cargo to various parts of the world. Tiny sailboats will often transfer bales of spices from one island to another, depending upon the port from which the spice is to be finally exported.

When next you lift a small box of cinnamon from your kitchen shelf to season an appetizer or a pie, or place a fragrant clove bud in a cup of piping hot tea, perhaps you'll recall much of the glamorous, romantic, and often dramatic history associ-ated with many of the spices. You even may imagine that you can see the tanned face of the lithe native boy who nimbly climbed the gigantic, tropical clove tree to pick the spicy un-opened flower bud for you. Or again, in imagination, you may feel the warm breath of the tropical breezes softly blow across your cheeks. You may imagine you hear the distant echoing of the majestic tones of Solomon the King as he invoked: "Awake, O north wind; and come, thou south; blow upon my garden, that the spices thereof may flow out."

SOURCES OF SPICES

Spices are the dried preparations of many a different plant. The product we call a spice may have been a piece of sweet-smelling bark, such as cinnamon; the seed of a luscious fruit, such as the nutmeg; an aromatic root like ginger or turmeric; a green berry like the fruit we call pepper; or an unopened flower bud, such as the clove.

The majority of the plants and trees from which we gather the roots, fruits, or barks for spices are of tropical origin and may not be cultivated in our temperate climate. However, I am including some information on their cultivation and harvesting for the sake of interest and because this book is designed as a companion to a previous volume, *The Art of Cooking with Herbs and Spices.*

When a specific herb or spice is adaptable to our North American continent and the experiments have proved it can be successfully grown in the warmer sections, the individual instructions for cultivating and harvesting are given in this volume. For example, the ginger plant is extensively grown on the island of Jamaica and in the subtropical section of Florida; and turmeric on the island of Haiti. Also specific suggestions are given for cultivating the various peppers which are ground to produce cayenne pepper and paprika. In the South and Southwest, especially in South Carolina, Texas, and New Mexico, the sesame plant is being developed under the supervision of the horticulturist, J. A. Martin, so that sesame is becoming a valuable commercial crop. See also Sesame Seed.

> *A fountain of gardens, a well of living waters, and streams from Lebanon. Awake, O north wind; and come, thou south; blow upon my garden, that the spices thereof may flow out.*
>
> —SOLOMON'S SONG

ALLSPICE, *Pimenta officinalis,* is the dried green fruit or berry of a beautiful 40-foot-high tropical evergreen tree which belongs to the myrtle, *Myrtaceae,* family. Allspice is the one major spice which is native to the West Indies and Central America. It is not adaptable to cultivation in the East Indies, and every experiment there which has been attempted has failed.

The tree, the *Pimenta karst,* is extensively cultivated on the island of Jamaica, and for this reason the tiny allspice berries are often referred to as JAMAICA PEPPER and JAMAICA PIMENTO. Mexico also cultivates the *Pimenta karst* trees and exports the allspice berries, but their quality is inferior to the Jamaica allspice.

The berry takes its name from the aroma and flavor, which resemble a combination of the fragrances of cloves, cinnamon, and nutmeg carefully blended. The green berry, an almost perfect miniature globe, is about ¼ inch in diameter. When dried, the allspice berry turns a reddish-brown.

Trees slow to mature: It takes 7 years for the *Pimenta karst* to mature and produce berries. However, after this long period of preparation nature compensates the grower, for the trees will bear fruit for 50 years or more.

The berries are usually harvested during July and August, after they have attained full growth but are still green in color. Native lads climb the trees and swing nimbly through the branches like young Tarzans, breaking off the small twigs which bear the fruits in clusters. The young boys throw the twigs to the ground as native women and children pick them up to sort them. The green berries are placed in one basket and the ripe berries in another. Only the green berries are selected for the preparation of the spice. The black, ripe berries are rather sweet and are not used for drying and grinding into allspice.

When the green berries have been separated they are placed in the sun and dried from 6 to 10 days. During the drying process the berries gradually change their color to a dark reddish-brown. The surface of the hard berry is rough when looked at under a microscope because of the tiny oil cells which cover it. Each berry holds 2 tiny kidney-shaped seed, but it is the pericarp covering which holds the real allspice flavor.

Uses: Both the whole and the ground allspice berries are used as seasoning in *pickles, meats, gravies, spice blends, curry powder, pastry spices, pickling spices,* and in the manufacture of *sausages* and *prepared meats. Potpourris, sweet scents,* and *sachets* make use of both the whole and the ground berries.

The ground spice lends a warm, sweet flavor to many foods such as *cakes, cookies,* baked *meat loafs, pies, salads, soups,* and *vegetables.* The Sicilians prepare an allspice-flavored, large, hard, round, savory cheese called *pepato.* It is sold in specialty stores and cheese markets. The whole allspice berries are left in the cheese and give it an extremely delicious and individual flavor. As one cuts through the cheese with a sharp knife, the tiny berries appear as little round, flavorful disks scattered through the slices, much as whole peppers appear in the paper-thin slices of a salami or Italian smoked sausage.

In Jamaica the whole allspice berry is considered an exotic

substitute for tobacco. There are specially designed long-stemmed allspice pipes. Those who have smoked the dried, fragrant berry say that its flavor is a delight unknown to tobacco smokers. Occasionally a sweet cordial is prepared from the berries which has a fragrant, distinctive flavor.

CASSIA, *Cinnamomum cassia blume,* or Chinese cinnamon bark, as it is often called, has been a valuable spice for centuries. Earlier than 2700 B.C. cassia was known and valued in the Orient. The majority of cinnamon which is used in America today is the bark of the cassia, for it is stronger in flavor than the true cinnamon, *Cinnamomum zeylanicum Nees,* which is native to Ceylon and India. See also Cinnamon or True Cinnamon.

Cassia barks vary greatly in thickness and color. The thin barks are usually smooth and have a warm, rich, dark brown color. The thicker barks are often a much lighter color and have rough surfaces. The quills or sticks which result from the peeling of the barks may be from 6 inches to 2 feet long, depending upon the variety, and as much as 1½ inches in diameter and from $\frac{1}{32}$ to ¼ inch in thickness.

Spice popular names: A spice often takes its popular name from the name of the port from which it is exported, and sometimes from the region where it is cultivated. CHINA CASSIA is native to China and Burma. It is cultivated widely throughout South China and is the bark from the evergreen tree, the *Cinnamomum cassia blume.* The thickness of the bark ranges from $\frac{1}{64}$ to $\frac{1}{16}$ of an inch, and when peeled the quills or sticks are from ⅜ to ¾ inch in diameter and from 1 to 2 feet long. It is a deep reddish-brown and when ground is a lighter reddish-brown.

The cassia cultivated in the northern part of French Indo-China is from another species of the *Lauraceae* family, the *Cinnamomum loureirii Nees.* Called SAIGON CASSIA, its taste is highly agreeable and it has a sweet, pungent aroma. This cassia has the best flavor of all the varieties which are imported. The ground spice from the thin bark is a light brown, while that from the thick bark is a much darker color with a slightly grayish tinge. The quills are from 6 to 12 inches long and as much as 1½ inches in diameter and ¼ inch thick.

The saigon cassia, though grown in Tonkin, is sent to Hong Kong and shipped from there.

There is a cassia native to the Dutch East Indies which is extensively cultivated in Java and on the island of Sumatra. The species to which this cassia, called BATAVIA CASSIA, belongs is somewhat doubtful. However, it is believed to be the *Cinnamomum Burmanni blume*. The popular name of the cassia is from the port of Batavia from which it is exported. When the bark is peeled the quills may be from 6 to 18 inches long, from ⅟₃₂ to ³⁄₁₆ inch thick, and almost ½ inch in diameter. The thin bark of the Batavia cassia is light yellowish-brown when ground; the thicker bark is a much darker brown.

The long, fancy quills or sticks of cassia are always left whole for export. They are graded as long, regular, and short. The small pieces of bark and trimmings which result from the packing are also graded for quality and appearance and carefully marked before shipping.

CASSIA BUDS are the dried, unripe fruit of two species of the *Cinnamomum:* the *Cinnamomum cassia* and the *Cinnamomum loureirii*. The tiny buds are from ¼ to ½ inch long and about ¼ inch wide at the crown. They taste sweet and spicy like the cassia barks.

Uses: Like the true cinnamon, both the whole stick and the ground cassia have many uses. The small pieces of bark are used in whole pickling spice blends and in the commercial manufacture of pickles and condiments; also in canned fruits and beverages. The ground cassia adds a distinctive sweet spiciness to many foods such as *buns, cakes, cookies, pies, fruits, desserts, meats, pickles, preserves, puddings, sauces, soups,* and *vegetables.*

The whole quills of cassia and the cassia buds are used in *potpourris* and *sachets;* and the oil of cinnamon has commercial value in the manufacture of *cosmetics* and *some perfumes.*

CAYENNE or **CAYENNE PEPPER,** *Capsicum,* is prepared by grinding varieties of the dried pods and the enclosed seed of the small-fruited *Capsicum* plants. The species belongs to the potato, *Solanaceae,* family.

Cayenne pepper should not be confused with either black pepper or white pepper. These peppers are the dried, whole berry or ground berry of the many varieties of an East Indian tropical plant or vine called the *Piper nigrum.*

The common name of the fruits or pods of the *Capsicum* plants from which cayenne is prepared is either RED PEPPERS or CHILIES. Many varieties of the chilies, native to tropical America, are now cultivated in all the warm climates in the world: in Africa, Asia, the East Indies, Hungary, Central America, South America, India, Italy, Japan, Mexico, the Southern United States, Spain, and also on the island of Zanzibar.

The records and history of our native *Capsicum* plants date back to the early fifteenth century. It was Chanca, the physician in the fleet of Columbus on his second voyage to America, who first wrote of an American spice he referred to as *agi* or *capsicum.* He recorded that the American Indians used *agi,* or *ají,* as a seasoning for the root vegetable called *age* or "yams." In the Spanish *agi* is still one of the common names for "Capsicum pepper."

Popular cayenne varieties: The small tapering red pepper pods or chilies, in sizes from ½ inch to 2 inches long and less than ½ inch wide, are the varieties most frequently used for grinding into cayenne pepper. The plants are the species known as the *Capsicum frutescens Linn* and the *Capsicum baccatum Linn.* The taste of the small fruits is very pungent, but the aroma of the ground pods and the seed is very sweet.

The Louisiana chili pepper, sometimes called by the popular name of the LOUISIANA SPORT PEPPER, is a beautiful shade of orange or deep red, and the flavor of the tiny, tapering fruit is extremely hot or pungent. See also other spices prepared from the varieties of the *Capsicum* plants: Chili Powder, Paprika, and Pepper or Red Pepper.

Warm-weather plants: The small-fruited *Capsicums* are shrubby perennials which are sensitive to cool weather. In fact, all the *Capsicums* need as much attention in cultivating as do the tomato plants. They require more heat and moisture than tomatoes and a much richer soil. The red peppers or chilies must be kept growing continuously and rapidly and for this reason are distinctly warm-weather plants. Unless the garden space is large and the summer is certain to be a long, warm one, it is perhaps wisest not to include the chilies in a small garden. If, however, one loves to pamper plants and there will be no occasion to neglect them, a dozen chili plants will be a worth-while additional small crop in the garden.

Cultivating: The *Capsicums* are slow to germinate and need to be planted in a hotbed with the soil temperature ranging from 70° F. to 75° F. for the first 12 to 15 days. After the germination period the temperature should be kept between 65° F. and 75° F.

Plenty of light with moderate moisture and good ventilation which does not allow the temperature to drop below 65° F. will produce healthy, stocky seedlings.

The seedlings should be kept in the hotbed about 12 or 15 days, or about 30 days from the date the seed is sown. Then they may be transplanted into the cold frame to become stronger. The temperature of the cold frame should be from 70° F. to 75° F. during the daytime and should not be allowed to drop below 60° F. at night. When placed in the cold frame, the seedlings should be partially shaded to keep them from wilting.

When ready to transplant into the garden, the young plants should be carefully blocked with a cube of the soil clinging to their roots and placed in the permanent location with them.

The chilies are grown commercially in several of our Southern and Southwestern states, including South Carolina, Louisiana, southern New Jersey, California, New Mexico, and Texas.

Harvesting: The matured red pepper pods are picked when firm and may be strung together by their individual stems. Hang in a warm, well-ventilated place to dry. Use as desired.

Uses: Whole chilies. The tiny, fiery whole chilies are placed in *sauces* and some blends of *pickling spices*. They are one of the chief ingredients in Tabasco sauce and other pungent prepared sauces.

Ground chilies. The cayenne pepper which results from the grinding of the dried chilies may be used in place of any of the other peppers as a seasoning for foods and sauces. However, it must be used with great discretion and care. Cayenne pepper is also one of the ingredients in some of the more pungent curry blends and chili powders.

CHILI POWDER is a blend of the dried ground pods of several varieties of Mexican chili peppers which belong to the species of plants called the *Capsicum,* a member of the potato, *Solanaceae,* family.

Various chili powders may or may not contain other powdered herbs and spices, though most blends usually include a small amount of ground cumin seed and orégano. The powder is prepared from a blend of any of the small, very hot and the larger, sweeter Mexican chilies, of which there are a large variety. Among the most popular are the MEXICAN CHILTEPIN, the CHILEPIQUINE, the CHILI PIQUIN, and the CHILE PETINE. All of these tiny, hot chilies are bright orange-red in color and average not more than ½ inch in length. The larger, sweeter varieties grow from 3 to 4½ inches long. The entire group of Mexican chilies comes under the botanical name of *Chile ancho,* var. *acuminatum.* See also other spices prepared from varieties of the *Capsicum* plants: Cayenne or Cayenne Pepper, Paprika, and Pepper or Red Pepper.

The flavor and aroma of a chili powder depend upon the manufacturer who has prepared the blend. There is a chili powder to satisfy every taste, from the mild varieties, which most Americans prefer, to the very hot blends of the Mexican and Spanish cuisines. Chili powder need not be pungent, and the judicious use of this dark red condiment is a most delightful addition to many foods.

Uses: Chili powder is flavorful in many other foods besides the traditional Aztec Indian dish of *chile con carne.* The spice adds a new tang to such foods as *eggs, meat marinades, Spanish rice, sauces, shellfish, soups,* and *sweet vegetables.*

CINNAMON or **TRUE CINNAMON,** *Cinnamomum zeylanicum Nees,* is the dried ground bark of any species of the evergreen tree, the *Cinnamomum,* which belongs to the laurel, *Lauraceae,* family.

The true cinnamon tree grows only in Ceylon and India. When the bark is ground, its flavor is delicate and sweet and the color is a yellowish-brown. See also Cassia.

Cinnamon is one of the oldest spices ever used by man. Its long and romantic history can be traced back to 5000 B.C. The Egyptians and ancient Hebrews used scented cinnamon oils in the sacred ceremonies and rituals in their temples and tabernacles. Cinnamon is still the predominant scent of the incense used in the cathedrals and churches of the world.

From Arabia the traders brought cinnamon to the Romans. Centuries later Milton immortalized the romantic history of the wandering spice caravans in the beautiful lines of his *Paradise Lost:* "Sabean odours from the spicie shoare of Arabie the blest . . ." The Arab traders jealously guarded the secret of the source of the cinnamon bark. They invented fabulous and fantastic stories of the difficulties they endured to secure the precious bark. They wished to keep control of the trade in this appealing and warmly scented spice, the expensive commodity of monarchs, as long as they possibly could.

The Romans dedicated this priceless product of commerce to Mercury, the God of Commerce, and burned the precious incense in his temples. The warm, sweet fragrance of cinnamon was believed also to influence the heart, and it was an ingredient in every *love potion* during the days of ancient superstitions.

Tropical bushy tree: In Ceylon the cultivated tree is small and bushy. The shiny leaves are a bright green and sweetly aromatic like the bark. The trees may be raised in nurseries from seed and then transplanted, or shoots from full-grown trees may be set out. In sandy soil the shoots will develop to a height of 5 or 6 feet, and each bush will bear at least 3 shoots for peeling. The first peeling begins only when the tree is almost 6 years old.

The young leaves of the cinnamon tree are red, and as soon as the leaves have turned a dark green the shoots may be cut for peeling. After the first cutting, 5 or 6 shoots or branches may be cut off every second year.

The cutting usually begins sometime in May and may continue until August and begin again in November. But the production depends upon the monsoons and the heavy rains, for the quills are more easily rolled and prepared immediately after a rainfall.

The branches are taken to a shelter and carefully scraped by the natives; then the bark is removed in long sections. The bark is sorted, peeled, and trimmed into pipes, or quills. As the bark dries, the quills curl into small sticks about an inch in diameter. Skilled workers insert the smaller rolls of bark into the larger ones, tie them into bundles, and grade them for export according to size, color, thickness, and quality.

The first-grade quills are compound pieces which have been

skillfully joined endwise. These are from 36 to 42 inches long. The broken pieces of the compound cinnamon quills vary in length from 2 to 8 inches and are about 1 inch in diameter. These are called cinnamon quillings. The short trimmings which fall when the inner bark is trimmed are called cinnamon chips, and the small pieces of bark which are left over from the trimming process are called cinnamon featherings. All forms of bark are graded, baled, and carefully marked according to government standards for export.

Uses: Both the ground cinnamon and the cinnamon quills are used in *spice blends* and in *pickling spices, perfumes,* and *cosmetics.* The culinary uses of cinnamon as seasoning are limitless, ranging from *beverages, cakes,* and *buns* to *soups, sauces,* and *vegetables.* Cinnamon adds a warm, sweet flavor to many foods such as *appetizers, beverages, desserts, fruits, pickles, pies, preserves, puddings, sauces,* and *ice creams.*

CLOVES, *Caryophyllus aromaticus L.,* are the dried unopened flower buds of the stately evergreen clove tree which belongs to the myrtle, *Myrtaceae,* family and is native to the Dutch East Indies.

The name of the flower bud was given to it because of its resemblance to a small nail, and the Dutch call the clove the *kruidnagel* or *spice nail.* The bud measures from ½ to ¾ inch long, and the small round head at the end of the calyx is held in place by 4 small points or claws. The aroma is extremely pungent and warm, and the taste of the bud almost biting.

The Chinese, Persians, Greeks, and Romans were familiar with the spicy, rich brown little nail-shaped buds which at one time were so costly that nation fought with nation over the ownership of the tropical islands where the clove trees were first discovered.

In the Molucca Islands the natives plant a clove tree when a child is born. They believe that as the tree flourishes the life of the child will also succeed. If the tree dies, tragedy will follow the life of the child in whose honor the tree was planted.

During the Middle Ages cloves were used to sweeten and preserve foods, and many of the old fifteenth-century recipes mentioned cinnamon, cloves, and ginger.

Zanzibar—ancient and modern trading center: Early in the nineteenth century the cultivation of large clove forests was introduced on the island of Zanzibar and its sister island, Pemba. The venture was so successful that today Zanzibar supplies more than 80 per cent of the world's cloves. Zanzibar has its own Clove Growers' Association, and the island is the only place in the world whose whole economic structure is dependent upon the clove. The United States alone imports more than 6,500,000 pounds of cloves from these two romantic islands.

Situated in the Indian Ocean off the east coast of Africa, Zanzibar is about 54 miles long. The entire island is not more than 640 square miles. Pemba, the sister island, is 25 miles northeast of Zanzibar and is 42 miles long with an area of 380 square miles. These two islands comprise the major part of the dominion of His Highness the Sultan of Zanzibar, Seyyid Sir Khalifa bin Harub, G.B.E., G.C.M.G.

Zanzibar was a flourishing community when the Great Pyramid of the Egyptian King, Cheops, was being built near Gizeh. More than 3,700 years B.C. traders from faraway Hindustan came to the island. Today it is still more oriental than African, and some of the natives trace their ancestry back to those courageous Hindustani merchants.

Majestic trees blossom for a hundred years: Though Zanzibar supplies so much of the world's consumption of cloves, the trees are also cultivated in Amboyna, British Malaya, Ceylon, India, Madagascar, and Penang. During the seventh year the tree bears the first flowers, but from then on it may continue to bear them for almost a hundred years. Though the tree is very tall and majestic-looking, the branches are frail and slender. The flowers begin as tiny pale green shoots, and then the calyx, about ¾ inch long, becomes tinged with a delicate pink.

This is the time for picking the buds. When they are allowed to stay on the tree for a longer period, the buds open and the flower becomes fertilized and forms a seed. This is called *mother-of-clove* and is an inferior product in comparison to the perfect unopened bud. The buds grow in clusters of from 10 to 50 heads on a main stem.

Two harvests annually: There are two harvesting seasons each year. One from July to October, the other from December to January. Native men, women, and children pick the bunches of buds from the lower branches by hand. The men climb the trees or place ladders against the stronger trunks to reach the upper branches. With a hooked stick they draw the fragile, slender branches toward themselves and pick as many of the remote bunches of buds as is possible. The top branches are never reached because they are so inaccessible.

The bunches are spread on huge mats and the green buds are removed from the stems by hand by the workers as they squat on the mats. The buds are dried on mats spread in the sun, and if the weather is good it takes only 4 or 5 days. The pale green buds turn to a warm rich brown, with the head a paler brown. While drying, they are turned over at intervals. Should it rain, the buds must be covered with mats, which retards the process and causes the buds to shrink. But all the cloves are graded and marked for export, and those which have become pale and wrinkled are called *khokers*. The percentage of *khokers* in the best grades of cloves is held down to 2 per cent.

Uses: The scent of the whole cloves is so pleasant that this fragrant spice is practically always one of the ingredients in *sachets, pomanders,* and *potpourris.* Cosmetics and soaps are scented with cloves, and the ache of many a tooth has been stopped by an application of oil of cloves. The culinary uses of both the whole and the ground clove are numerous and varied. Clove adds a sweet pungency to many foods such as *appetizers, beverages, desserts, fruits, meats, pickles, preserves, puddings, sauces, soups,* and *sweet vegetables.* See also Sweet Scents and Sachets.

GINGER, *Zingiber officinale Roscoe,* with its large, brilliant flowers, is one of the most beautiful of all the tropical plants of nature. Native to southern Asia, the ginger plant, used in culinary art, is now extensively cultivated in tropical climates, including Puerto Rico, southern Florida, and especially on the island of Jamaica, from where we secure the highest quality of ginger.

The root or rhizome is the part of the plant which is prepared for use. It is wonderfully fragrant and pungently spicy whether the root is dried, crystallized, sugared, preserved, or ground into a fine powder. The root pieces are irregular in shape and vary in colors of buff and yellow with pungent or less pungent flavors, depending upon where the gingers have been grown. The three considered the best quality are the gingers which are grown in Africa, India, and the island of Jamaica.

Ginger was cultivated in the Orient centuries before Europe knew that the plant existed. One of the most ancient of spices, ginger was probably used by the Babylonians, for it is mentioned many times in the Talmud. And the botanical name as well as the common name was derived from the Old Sanskrit, the ancient Aryan language of India. Ginger in those early centuries was called ZINGEHER.

Marco Polo, in his fabulous tales of his travels in China during the thirteenth century, wrote glowing accounts of the cultivation of the ginger plants. The Spaniards brought ginger to the New World early in the sixteenth century; and as a result we still enjoy the superb flavor of the ginger which grows in Jamaica.

There are more than 275 species of the *zingiberaceous* plants. Among several of the first cousins are GALANGAL, *Alpinia galanga,* TURMERIC, *Curcuma longa,* and ZEDO-ARY, *Curcuma zedoaria.* Galangal was popular as a culinary spice in China and Europe about the ninth century. But today it is practically unknown except in Russia, where it still is used to flavor a liquor called *Nastoika.*

Zedoary was used extensively in condiments during the Middle Ages, but it has been almost completely obliterated by time. In some of the remote Far Eastern countries today the pungent aroma of zedoary still is used to scent oriental perfumes. Turmeric is the only relative of the ginger root which we still know and use as a flavoring. See also Turmeric.

Cultivating ginger plants in Florida: Ginger plants require a very fertile soil with good drainage, plenty of heavy rain, and high temperatures. That's why it thrives in the tropical and subtropical regions in both the Eastern and Western Hemispheres. The long, pinnate leafstalks branch out from the main stem and make a bushy-looking plant 3 or 4 feet high. The flowers develop in a conelike cluster of overlapping bracts. Each bract encloses from 1 to 3 blossoms. When the plant is a year old the stem withers and the roots or rhizomes are dug up. This perennial is easily propagated from small divisions of the rhizomes, which have at least one bud or "eye."

The experiments in Florida have been quite successful, and

there the divisions of rhizomes are planted in February. They are set about 3 inches deep, 16 inches apart, and in rows separated 2 feet. They grow quite fast, and the only cultivation necessary is a regular hoeing to keep the plants free of weeds. As the rhizomes enlarge, the upper plant develops leafstalks and then the flower stalks develop in the autumn. By December the roots or rhizomes may be harvested and prepared for use. The Florida experiments have not been developed to a commercial extent, for since the harvesting and preparation must all be done by hand, the cost of labor would probably make production economically impossible.

Plant takes 10 months to mature: The underground stem or rhizome of the ginger is dug up about 10 months after planting. The soil is shaken off, the withered tops cut off close to the rhizome, and all fibrous roots removed. The rhizomes grow in the form of several branches or fingers, and these are separated to facilitate the removing of all the soil.

For dried ginger there are two different treatments. If the ginger is to be exported unpeeled, it is merely washed thoroughly in scalding water and then dried in the sun. The unpeeled is called either BLACK GINGER or GREEN GINGER. If the rhizomes are to be shipped peeled, they are thoroughly washed and a thin layer of skin is very carefully peeled off by hand with a sharp knife. Finally the rhizomes are scalded in hot water and dried in the sun. This is called quite simply PEELED GINGER.

Preserved ginger in syrup: Preserved ginger is usually prepared from the young rhizomes which have not acquired their full pungency. The root is washed thoroughly and then meticulously peeled. Afterward it is boiled in a rich sugar or honey solution. The process of boiling or curing the rhizomes is repeated until they are thoroughly soaked in the rich syrup. They are then packed in crocks, jars, or tins, ready for export.

Uses: Ginger is undoubtedly one of our most valuable of spices. It has commercial worth in the preparation of medicines, and its culinary uses in foods and beverages are endless. In India, ginger tea is often served in place of the flower teas. We flavor *gingerbread, cakes, cookies, puddings, pies, sausages,* and *prepared meats* with ginger. *Ginger ale* and *ginger beer* are both favorite beverages. Many of the blended *pickling* and *pie spices* contain ginger root or ground ginger, and preserved ginger is an epicurean delight.

MACE or **TRUE MACE,** *Myristica fragrans Houtt,* is the aril or outer shell which covers the kernel of the fruit of a tall, luxuriant tropical tree called the nutmeg tree. See also Nutmeg.

The tropical fruits of the beautiful evergreen nutmeg are about the size of a small peach and equally as luscious. When the ripe fruits are split open, three layers of brilliant colors are revealed: a bright green, then orange, and finally the brilliant scarlet of the aril. This third layer or rough covering of the nutmeg kernel is called mace. When this protective cover is flattened and dried, it is called BLADES OF MACE or WHOLE MACE. When ground, the resulting powder is called GROUND or POWDERED MACE.

The island of Grenada: Though the nutmeg trees are native to the East Indies, they are now extensively cultivated in the British West Indies, especially on the island of Grenada. The nutmeg plantations on this island produce more than half the entire world's supply of nutmegs and mace. The nutmeg industry is the chief industry of the island, and more than 27,000 acres are planted in nutmeg groves.

Grenada is one of the islands in the West Indies discovered by Columbus in 1498. Today it is a regular port of call for several of the Canadian, English, French, and American transatlantic freighters and passenger ships from Montreal, London, and New York. It also has a modern airport near the harbor of St. George's on the blue Caribbean.

The French colonized Grenada during the seventeenth century, when it was held by the Carib Indians. However, the British took over in 1762 and again in 1783, and Grenada has remained British territory ever since.

Preparing mace: The crimson covering is carefully removed from the nutmeg kernel and then spread out in the sun to dry. In drying, the brilliant color changes to a pale reddish-brown or a yellowish-brown, and the aril becomes hard and brittle.

The best-flavored maces are those which come from the tropical island of Grenada, one of the most popular islands of the Windward Islands in the Lesser Antilles of the West Indies;

and from the Banda Islands in the Molucca Archipelago; also from Penang, the British island off the west coast of the Malay Peninsula. Both the aroma and the taste of the GRENADA MACE and all the true maces are fragrant and aromatic like the nutmeg.

Other maces: BOMBAY MACE or WILD MACE is not a true mace, and government standards require that it be accurately identified as "the dried arillus of *Myristica malabrica Lam.*" This tree is native to India and belongs to the *Myristica* family, a large genus of tropical trees which make up the nutmeg, *Myristicaceae,* family. All of the trees bear small white or yellow flowers and fleshy fruits with a hard seed enclosed in a vividly colored arillode. The covering or aril of the Bombay nutmeg is a dark reddish-brown. It is about 1½ inches long and looks like a tiny dome with elongated twigs or branches attached. It has very little fragrance and taste.

Other maces which reach the commercial markets and which are different from the true mace are the MACASSAR MACE and the PAPUA MACE. The former comes from Macassar on the southwest coast of the Celebes Island in the Dutch East Indies, and the Papua mace from the island of New Guinea. Both these maces are from the tropical tree, *Myristica agentea Warb.*, which is one of the many varieties of the nutmeg family.

Uses: Mace is used in combination blends of prepared spices such as *pie spices, poultry seasonings,* and *prepared meat* and *sausage spice blends.* When used alone, its flavor is similar to nutmeg but strong, and it is a most delicious ingredient in *cakes, cookies, pies, preserves,* and all *sweet baked goods.* Mace is also unusually tasty when used to season such foods as *appetizers, cheeses, fish, meats, salads, puddings, sauces, shellfish, stews, soups,* and *vegetables.*

MUSTARD or **DRY MUSTARD.** See Mustard Plant.

NUTMEG, *Myristica fragrans Houtt,* is the dried seed or nut found inside the kernel of the tropical fruit of the nutmeg tree. See also Mace or True Mace.

The grayish-brown nutmegs vary in size from ¾ inch to 1¼ inches in length and from ½ to ¾ inch in diameter. Some of the nutmegs are oval and others may be almost round. The aroma of the dried nut is pleasantly pungent, and when the spice is freshly ground it has a warm, peculiarly bitter taste which adds a luscious flavor to many foods and beverages.

The nutmeg tree belongs to the tropical *Myristicaceae* family which is native to the East Indian archipelago popularly referred to as the Spice Islands. Not only are the trees cultivated on the island of Grenada, but also in the Banda Islands, Ceylon, Java, Penang, Singapore, and Sumatra. All species of this large family of tropical evergreens have heavy, large, waxy leaves similar to those of our rhododendron plants. The colorful flowers of all the *Myristicaceae* family are white and yellow.

Luxuriant nutmeg groves: The groves of the tall nutmeg trees resemble orange groves in their color scheme, with their many blossoms and small, round green fruits which turn a golden yellow when ripe. The trees grow to a height of 20 or 25 feet. The fruits make most delicious jams, jellies, and conserves which have a warm, spicy flavor.

Nutmegs and mace from the same districts bear the same names of identification. For example, mace from Penang is called PENANG MACE, and nutmeg from Penang is called PENANG NUTMEG. They are graded for export as large, medium, and small, depending upon the number of nutmegs which will weigh a pound. It takes from 60 to 75 large nutmegs to make a pound; and from 100 to 110 of the small size to weigh that much.

Both nutmeg and mace are comparatively young spices in culinary history. Europe knew them first during the twelfth century. Before that time the Romans used burning nutmegs as a fragrant incense along the roads. By the time the Dutch had formed the Dutch East India Company in 1600, nutmegs had become an important item in world trade. Exportation from the Netherlands Indies was limited except through government channels in an effort to continue high prices. To carry out the order, the Dutch carefully guarded the islands, and the nutmegs which were exported were dipped in lime to kill their fertility. But both the French and the English managed to smuggle out amounts of unlimed nutmegs for cultivation on their islands. Legend tells us that large birds, attracted by the fragrant fruit and the crimson cover of the mace, also carried off the whole fruits. As they ate the fruit and the mace, the seed was dropped in far-off places and took root and grew.

The Nutmeg State: When the Dutch were in control of the spice trade, American ingenuity stepped in and has given us a legend. It says that our Connecticut Yankees carved nutmegs out of wood, dipped them in lime, and actually sold some of them to the Dutch. True or not, it is a tribute to their sense of humor. And Connecticut certainly earned its nickname of *The Nutmeg State* through a clever and amusing intrigue.

The Malayans love their nutmeg trees and say that the trees cannot bear their luscious fruits unless they are planted where they can hear the sound of the sea in their branches and feel the nourishment of animal food at their feet. There is something to this idea, for the trees which are nearest the sea and grow in the richest soil and have the most care are the ones which bear the choicest fruits.

Nutmeg matures after 9 years: The kernels with the seed are from the fertilized female trees only.

It takes 9 years for the nutmeg tree to mature after planting, and 6 or 7 years of normal growth before the sexes are noticeable. The male trees, whose flower pollen has fertilized the female flowers, are then cut down to allow room for the planting of more trees. Now, branches of the fertile female trees are grafted on all plants. When these grafted trees are but 2 years old, their sex can be easily distinguished. After the mature trees begin bearing fruit, they will continue doing so for as long as 50 years if properly cared for and fertilized.

The natives gather the nutmegs by means of a long pole which has prongs and a basket attached. The prongs loosen the fruit, letting it fall into the basket, which the natives call a *gai gai*. When gathered, the outer husk is discarded and the aril or mace is separated from the seed; then both are dried. It takes several weeks of drying in the hot sun before the nut begins to rattle around. The kernels are opened and the nutmeg drops out.

Uses: The delicate flavor of nutmeg is used in many formulas of the *prepared spice blends*, for *pie spices, poultry seasonings,* and *prepared meat seasonings.* Nutmeg is always used in *spice cakes, cookies,* and *fruit pies.* The spice adds a pungent flavor to *chutneys, stewed fruits, meats, puddings, fruit-salad dressing, sauces, soups, vegetables,* and various *milk drinks.*

PAPRIKA, *Capsicum annum Linn,* is the spice or condiment which is prepared from the ripe dried pods of the larger and sweeter varieties of the *Capsicum* plant. See also other spices prepared from varieties of the *Capsicum* plant: Cayenne, or Cayenne Pepper, Chili Powder, Pepper or Red Pepper.

Paprika varies in color, flavor, and pungency, depending upon the exact variety of the sweet pepper from which it is ground. The choicest grades of paprika are prepared from the best-quality pods, which have been carefully selected. All stems, stalks, and *placentae* are discarded, but the seed of the pods are also ground with the fleshy part of the pod. The color of the highest-quality paprika is a rich, dark red.

The rose paprika, also called HUNGARIAN PAPRIKA, is prepared in Hungary from the choicest of sweet pods. Its rich color and sweet aroma are distinctive and the flavor mildly pungent. KING'S PAPRIKA, also called KOENIGSPA-PRIKA, is prepared from the entire pepper with the stem, which makes its flavor much sharper.

The Spanish and Portuguese, as well as the Mexicans, prepare varieties of paprika suitable to their individual tastes. They are usually more pungent than either the Hungarian or the American paprikas.

Uses: Many of the world's various cuisines use this spice so rich in vitamin C. The French, Spanish, Mexican, Portuguese, Hungarian, and American homemakers use paprika both as a *seasoning* and as a *decoration* for many foods such as *appetizers, cheeses, eggs, fish, shellfish, game, meats, poultry, salads, soups, stews,* and *vegetables.*

PEPPER or **BLACK PEPPER,** *Piper nigrum L.,* is the whole or ground dried berry of one of the varieties of the tropical vine, *Piper nigrum.* There are more than a thousand species of this woody vine, native to the East Indies, and the plant is widely cultivated in those islands as well as in Siam, Thailand, and India. See also Pepper or White Pepper.

Pepper as a Roman ransom: Pepper was the most valued and expensive of all the staple commodities of trade in ancient times. It was known and used by the Greeks centuries before

Christ and was frequently demanded as payment for taxes. This most noble of spices was one of the tributes demanded by Alaricus (376–410), King of the Visigoths, Conqueror of Rome. The ransom for the beautiful city of seven hills was set at 5,000 pounds of gold, 30,000 pounds of silver, and 3,000 pounds of pepper. Needless to say, the pepper in those days was far more difficult to secure than gold and silver. Even today pepper is 2500 per cent higher in price than it was ten years ago.

The Pepper Exchange: All during the Middle Ages pepper remained the chief staple commodity of trade between India and Europe. Early in the tenth century English landlords taxed their tenants one pound of pepper annually. By the early part of the twelfth century the pepper trade had become so valuable and important that England formed the "Gild of Pepperers," a combination labor and trading organization. This first "gild" might be called one of the main forerunners of any number of our modern unions and trade exchanges. The New York Pepper Exchange, organized in 1937, has helped make the United States the world's greatest importer, exporter, and consumer of pepper. We alone use more than 35,000,000 pounds of this valuable, fragrant spice every year.

Trade names: There are many black peppers which are exported; and they, like the other spices, take their specific names from the districts where they have been cultivated, or the names of the ports from which they are shipped. Among those names best known to the trade are Alleppey, Java, Johore, Lampong, Penang, Saigon, Siam, Singapore, Tellicherry, and Trang.

Verdant pepper vines bear fruit twice a year: The luxuriant, woody vine-plant grows rapidly either from seed or from vine cuttings. Each vine is supported by wooden posts about 12 feet high. As soon as the plant is 3 feet high it is released from the post and wound around the bottom of it close to the ground. The vine is then carefully and completely covered with soil. This treatment produces more shoots, until finally the plant completely obliterates the tall wooden post with a dense mass of branches.

The plant bears some fruit during the first year, but it is not really fully developed until the third or fourth. From then on the plant produces two crops a year for about 18 years. The crops are harvested during March and April, and again during August and September. The latter crops are always larger than those of March and April. After bearing for 18 years the plant gradually begins to weaken. When it no longer blossoms the vine is dug up and replaced by new shoots.

Each flower spike holds about 50 berries which do not ripen all at the same time. First the berry is green, then yellow, and finally red. The ripe red berries are detached from the spikes by hand and gathered into baskets. The red berries are dried in the sun, either on the ground or suspended in huge mats and herb-smoked, depending upon where the plant is grown. For example, the LAMPONG BLACK PEPPER berries are dried on the ground, while the Singapore pepper berries are dried on huge mats suspended over kettles in which the *Gambier* shrub is boiled. The herb-scented smoke from the kettles flavors the pepper berries and turns them black. Pepper dried in this manner has a superior flavor to that which has been dried on the ground.

Characteristics: The dried pepper berry is almost a perfect little globe covered with innumerable wrinkles. The berry or peppercorn measures less than ¼ inch in diameter, and it takes about 500 of the average-sized peppercorns to weigh an ounce. The color, depending upon how the berry is dried, ranges from dark brown to black, and the aroma is penetrating and somewhat sweetish. See also Pepper or White Pepper.

Whole berry called PEPPERCORN. To secure the best flavor from the pepper berries, the whole pepper should be freshly ground in a pepper mill at the exact moment it is being used to season the food. Formerly all our pepper mills were manufactured abroad, chiefly in France, where the French have always been aware of the deliciously fragrant aroma and fresh tasty pungency of newly ground pepper. In addition to a variety of English- and Italian-made pepper mills, there are a number of excellent American-made mills of high quality and artistic design. Among both the imported and the American ones which have come to my attention, I find that the *Olde Thompson* pepper mills are superior in quality, artistic imagination, and durability.

Uses: Pepper as a seasoning is as universally popular as salt, if not more so. The whole peppercorns are used to flavor many prepared meats and sausages. Pickling spices, marinades, and condiments make use of both the black and white varieties. All foods, except our sweet desserts, are enhanced by the use of this most fragrant and tasty of spices. The tremendous and lucrative production of the peppercorns in the Dutch East Indies alone averages as much as 80,000,000 pounds annually.

PEPPER or **RED PEPPER,** *Capsicum,* belongs to the family of chilies and is not related to either the black or white peppers. See also other spices prepared from varieties of the *Capsicum* plants: Cayenne or Cayenne Pepper, Paprika, and Chili Powder.

The name red pepper may refer to cayenne pepper which is ground, or it may be a pungent, whole dried red pepper pod. However, in this case, it is considered as the CRUSHED RED PEPPER used for culinary seasoning in foods and sauces. It consists of the dried crushed pods of the large variety of hot chilies with the whole unground seed. Red pepper is also labeled PEPERONE ROSSO.

Characteristics: Crushed red pepper has an unusually pungent aroma with a flavor which is spicy and biting. The tiny, flat, almost round seed are a rich golden yellow and the crushed pod a deep orange or red.

Uses: The Spaniards and Mexicans use the crushed red pepper as a seasoning in many of their main foods more than any other nationality except perhaps the Italians. They rarely prepare a tomato sauce without this fiery little condiment. Used with care and judgment, crushed red pepper adds a delicious tang to *stewed vegetables, meats,* and *sauces.*

PEPPER or **WHITE PEPPER,** *Piper nigrum L.,* is prepared from the dried black peppercorns, which are the dried mature fruits of any of the many varieties of the *Piper nigrum* plants or vines. See also Pepper or Black Pepper.

Characteristics: The white peppercorn is always smaller than the black peppercorn and quite smooth. Its light yellowish-gray color is achieved by peeling off the rough outer surfaces of the dried black peppercorns. This is done by soaking the black peppercorns in water and brushing or peeling off the softened outer hulls. When the process is a mechanical one it is called decortication, and the highest quality of white peppercorns prepared this way are identified as decorticated white pepper. England prepares or manufactures the best white pepper, and limited quantities of a super grade also reach us from Leghorn, Italy.

Uses: Whole white peppercorns are especially attractive and useful in the pepper mills which grind out the desired amount of seasoning during mealtimes. The aroma and the flavor of the white peppercorns, however, are not as strong and fragrant as those of the black peppercorns since several coatings of the black berry have been peeled off. However, white pepper may be used more freely than the black for this reason and also because its appearance on light-colored foods and in white sauces is more appealing. Both the whole white peppercorns and the ground white pepper may be used with all the foods with which one naturally uses black pepper.

> *A garden inclosed is my sister, my spouse; a spring shut up, a fountain sealed. Thy plants are an orchard of pomegranates, with pleasant fruits; camphire, with spikenard, Spikenard and saffron; calamus and cinnamon, with all trees of frankincense; myrrh and aloes, with all the chief spices.*
>
> —SONG OF SOLOMON

SAFFRON, or **SAFFRON POWDER,** *Crocus sativus,* is the most delicately perfumed of all the spices. The golden powder, made from the stigmas of this charming little autumn crocus, has been used as a household luxury and has been a part of history from the time of our earliest records right through to modern times without interruption.

The slender green leaves and pale purple flowers of this autumn crocus are known in all parts of southern Europe, Asia, the Far East, and America. Though native to southern Europe and Asia, the *Crocus sativus* is extensively cultivated at present in Austria, France, Greece, Spain, Sicily, and the countries of the Far East.

In the United States this crocus has been grown as a small garden crop in Lancaster and Lebanon counties in Pennsylvania. However, the production of saffron hasn't been developed commercially in America because the process of harvesting is such an expensive one. Each crocus blossom has 3 saffron stigmas. The blossoms must be picked by hand, then each of the 3 delicate filaments also must be picked off by hand. Since it takes 75,000 hand-picked blossoms to supply enough stigmas for one pound of saffron, it is small wonder that saffron was the symbol of luxury and extravagance during the early days of the Roman Empire.

Golden saffron—the plant of the sun: The rich, golden hue of the saffron was acclaimed as the color of kings and monarchs and the plant designated as "the plant of the sun." Solomon treasured its perfumed beauty in his gardens, as did the Babylonians. Nero's chariot wheels rolled along the saffron-sprinkled roads of glamorous Rome as the triumphant conqueror made his entry into the Eternal City.

The Greeks, Romans, and Hebrews used the sweet-scented saffron powder, dissolved in water, as a spray for their theaters and banquet halls. The Egyptians called saffron "The Blood of Thoth" and worshiped this god of wisdom and magic by burning the sweet powder during all their religious ceremonies. As a special sacrifice to the gods, they would blend the expensive golden powder with frankincense and myrrh.

From India and Arabia the use of saffron powder in foods was introduced in Spain. The Crusaders brought saffron with them into England and France, and more than a third of all the medieval recipes refer to its luxurious use. Saffron was so expensive that it could be used only in the households of the wealthy and in the palaces of kings. Today America imports more than 3,000 pounds of this precious golden-yellow seasoning for culinary use.

Uses: True saffron powder is a must in many favorite recipes of the French, Hindustani, Italian, and Spanish cuisines. A small amount of the golden powder is sufficient as a flavoring for *breads, cakes, cookies, fish* and *shellfish stews,* and exotic *sauces.* Saffron gives a lovely color to pale sauces and makes a cake more attractive as well as adding its subtle saffron taste.

The powder of the Mexican saffron is used as a substitute or an adulterant for the true saffron. The red florets are used chiefly as coloring in alkaline dyes, cosmetics, liqueurs, and candies. The fruit of the safflower, sometimes referred to as a seed, is crushed to produce an oil which is used in India both for cooking and for burning in lamps.

Cultivating: True saffron. This *Crocus sativus,* which belongs to the iris family, will grow in practically all temperate
climates. It is much quicker to the day of blossoming if one
buys the plants or corms of this bulbous flower, since it takes
3 years for the plant to bear blossoms if planted from seed.

A rich, well-drained soil will give a vigorous-looking plant,
but the best-quality saffron is obtained from the flowers which
have grown in soil of only medium fertility. The corms may
be planted in August in furrows 6 inches deep and set 4 inches
apart in parallel rows separated about 20 inches. Then the
furrows are filled and the ground made level. The soil must
be well cultivated and kept free from weeds at all times.
Though the blossoms will appear in October, the main leaf
growth follows in the next spring.

The corms or bulbs may be left in the ground 2 or 3 years
before taken up and divided. However, like other bulb plants,
they may be dug up each year and subdivided. If this is done,
they should be frequently checked for a fungus growth which
may attack the bulbs. All unsound bulbs should be detached
to prevent the fungus growth from spreading to the good
bulbs.

The SAFFLOWER or MEXICAN SAFFRON, also called
FALSE SAFFRON, is an annual which is unrelated to the true
saffron, though the powder of the safflower is sometimes used
as a substitute for the true saffron. The safflower is the *Car-
thamus tinctorius L.,* which is native to Egypt and the Mediterranean countries and is cultivated in the temperate regions
of America, England, and Mexico. The plant grows from
1 to 2 feet high with smooth, alternate, shiny, lance-ovate
leaves which branch out from the main stem. The orange-
colored flowers resembling thistles have a 5-cleft corolla, and
the tiny orange-red florets are dried separately to produce
either a golden yellow or a red powder.

This saffron is very easy to cultivate in warm, sunny places.
The seed germinate quickly and the mature plants may be
spaced at 6 inches. However, when planted in groups, they
make a bright, brilliant spot in the garden. The soil should be
light and the plants kept well cultivated until they are in full
bud.

Harvesting: True saffron. In October, as soon as the blossoms
appear, they should be picked daily as they open. The blossom-

ing period usually lasts about 3 weeks. The orange-colored stigmas are removed from the flowers by pulling each one out by hand. The flowers are then thrown away. The stigmas should be dried immediately by placing them on a very fine sieve suspended over a low fire so they may dry quickly. Then they are placed in linen bags and stored in a dry place until powdered. The stigmas may also be powdered as soon as dried and the saffron powder packed in tightly corked bottles ready to be used.

TURMERIC, *Curcuma longa L.,* is a member of the brilliant tropical ginger, *Zingiberaceae,* family. Turmeric, although native to tropical Asia and China, is also cultivated in the West Indies, especially on the island of Haiti.

The turmeric plant of the genus *Curcuma* changes its appearance, depending upon the section in which it is grown. When cultivated in China, the flowers and foliage take on a dull green color, but in the East Indies its flowers are a brilliant orange color. See also Ginger.

Like the ginger plant, it is the aromatic root or rhizome of the turmeric which is washed, dried, and then ground into the spice. The perennial root is rough on the surface with rings or ridges encircling it. One part of the root is sometimes called long-fingered turmeric because of its slender shape. Other pieces of the irregular root are bulbous, and still others may curve slightly and taper to a point at one end. The roots are about the same size as the ginger root and may vary in length from 1 to 4 inches and are about ½ inch in thickness.

Varieties of turmeric: The color of the ground turmeric varies from a pure light yellow to a deeper orange-yellow, depending upon the districts where the root has grown and the processes of drying and grinding. The ALLEPPEY TURMERIC, which is exported from the port of Alleppey in the district of Travencore, India, is a warm orange-yellow, while MADRAS TURMERIC is a light lemon-yellow. HAITI TURMERIC is much darker than any of the East Indian and Chinese varieties. Its color is a deep, rich, dark orange tinged with yellow. The spice imparts a distinctly rich taste, color, and flavor to curry powder, of which it is a main ingredient.

This colorful relative of the ginger plant is cultivated and harvested much as the tropical ginger. The root divisions are set in rows separated at least 2 feet. As the root develops, the upper plant puts out its leaf and flower stalks. When the plant has matured and withered, the root is dug up, washed, and spread under the tropical sun to dry. The pieces are frequently turned so they will dry evenly. The process in good weather takes from a week to 10 days. When the moisture in the root has been reduced and the root is quite brittle, it is ready to be ground into fine powder.

Uses: Today turmeric is used chiefly as a culinary seasoning, though this ancient spice was regarded also as a perfume during biblical times. In India turmeric is among the favored spices and is always used in preparing *curry blends* and *condiments*. It has a sweet, somewhat tangy flavor and adds a beautiful color to the foods and spice blends in which it is used. Sometimes a mustard blend is given a deeper color by using turmeric as an adulterant. The whole root as well as the ground spice is equally delicious in flavoring *pickles* and *relishes*. Some East Indian recipes will suggest the use of turmeric in place of the more expensive saffron powder.

This most useful of spices is flavorful in many foods such as *cakes, cookies, curry blends, fish* and *shellfish, salad dressings, meats, pickles, poultry, relishes,* and *sauces.*

CHAPTER NINE

Herb and Spice
Sweet Scents
and Sachets

Sweet scents and sachets, pomanders and rose jars, lotions and moth preventives take on a new significance when they are blended and prepared at home. The sweet fragrance of the sachet or the spicy and herby aroma of the potpourri can reflect the personality and preferences of the blender. A scent or a perfume is a highly personal expression under any circumstances. And when a special fragrance has been blended from the flowers and herbs which have blossomed in a familiar garden, the effect of the mingled sweet scents in the home can be almost mystical.

One sudden whiff of a perfumed sachet or of the subtle fragrance which comes into a room as the cover of a rose jar is lifted to release the warm scent of roses from a special garden can stir up multicolored memories. A remembered even faint fragrance can bring into vividness the majestic beauty of June nights or reincarnate the thrilling stimulation of the warm sunshine of forgotten summer mornings. In a split second a particular favorite perfume can revive in the consciousness the happenings of remote times and faraway places.

Harriet Ware, the American composer and poetess, once experienced a most unusual effect of the sudden whiff of a long-forgotten fragrance. She told me that upon this particular occasion, when visiting in the home of a much-traveled friend, she had noticed an especially beautiful antique rose jar on the grand piano. The exquisiteness of its design attracted her attention. She commented on its delicate beauty to her friend, who suggested that she open the jar to enjoy also the fragrance of its perfumed petals. Miss Ware opened the lovely jar, and almost instantaneously words and music began singing in her heart and mind. She hurried home to write one of the most beautiful poems of her entire career and composed another gem of a song which she named "From India," for the rose jar had come from there.

The opening lines of the lovely song express what happened to Miss Ware when the fragrance of the rose petals filled the room. The lines begin: "In this ancient jar from India are memories and rose leaves from a moonlit garden long ago. Drifting on their haunting perfume comes the music of the fountain, and your voice, Beloved, hushed for years."

Rose jars, potpourris, and sachets may not inspire you to poetry and song, but they can give you and all of us a deep and genuine pleasure in the mere gathering of the petals and in the preparation of the blending of the spices. Long after the blossoming herbs and flowers have gone, the scent of the rose jars and the sweet-smelling sachets will bring to your rooms for many months to come the freshness and fragrance of your summer garden.

The suggested combinations in the following pages are included as a guide to the preparing of your own specially selected scents. Take those sweetly scented herbs and heavily perfumed roses which are your favorites, and the results will reflect you and your particular tastes and inclinations.

> *Take unto thee sweet spices . . . these sweet spices with pure frankincense: of each shall there be a like weight: And thou shalt make it a perfume . . . after the art of the apothecary.*
>
> —EXODUS 30:34, 35

CULINARY HERBS FOR FRAGRANT LOTIONS

Balm, Lemon	Mints	Rosemary
Basil, Sweet	Rose Geranium	Verbena, Lemon
Lavender		

CULINARY HERBS AND SPICES IN FRAGRANT
MOTH-PREVENTIVE BLENDS

Allspice	Lavender	Spearmint
Cinnamon	Peppermint	Tansy
Cloves	Rosemary	Woodruff, Sweet
Ginger		

Also Patchouli Leaves, Sandalwood, Southernwood, Winter Bark, Wormwood, Dried Lemon and Orange Peel

HERBS AND SPICES FOR SWEET SCENTS, SACHETS, AND
POTPOURRI BLENDS

Allspice	Ginger	Rose Buds
Anise	Lavender	Rose Petals
Balm, Lemon	Mace	Rosemary
Basil, Sweet	Mints	Sage
Cinnamon	Nutmeg	Thyme
Coriander		Verbena, Lemon

Also Hops and Melilot or Sweet Clover

CHAPTER TEN

Recipes

for Household Uses

of Herbs and Spices

Attar of Roses   TIME: Variable

Rose Petals   *Coarse salt*

The fragrant petals of the damask rose, *Rosa damascena,* are usually the most satisfactory for distilling attar of roses; but any fragrant variety may be used.

Select only the fresh unbruised leaves of roses which have been picked after all dew has evaporated, but which are still filled with fragrance and contain the greatest amount of volatile oil.

Place a layer of fresh leaves in a clean crock or earthen jar which may be tightly covered. Over each layer sprinkle a thin covering of salt; repeat until the crock is full. Cover tightly; place crock in cool, dark spot; in a cellar if possible. Allow to stand 6 weeks without disturbing.

Strain and press moisture through filter cloth. Pour essence into a transparent bottle; cork tightly. Stand in the sun for 6 weeks to purify.

One drop of this attar of roses will perfume a pint of water.

Rose Petal Pearls   TIME: 4 hours or more

Petals of red roses   *Infinite patience*

Collect the velvety petals of excessively fragrant fresh red roses and place in an iron mortar. Crush and beat the beautiful fresh petals for at least 2 hours with a pestle, or until the petals form a thick, fragrant paste.

Roll ½ teaspoon of the paste into a tiny bead; set aside on a clean tray or screen; allow to stand in a warm, airy spot until the beads become thoroughly dried and hard.

Polish each tiny bead with a soft cloth.

Use as *sachet beads* in lingerie and linens.

Each bead retains the full fragrance of fresh roses touched with dew.

Rose Petal Potpourri   TIME: Variable

Rose petals
Coarse salt
¼ oz. dried orris root
¼ oz. ginger
¼ oz. ground cloves
1 small stick cinnamon, crushed

¼ oz. nutmeg
¼ oz. allspice
4 tbs. dried lemon verbena leaves
5 drops oil of jasmine

Gather fresh unbruised petals of several varieties of roses after dew has dried but before roses have lost their fragrance. Separate petals carefully; spread on clean cloth or screen to dry in shade for 3 or 4 days. Use about 1 quart dried petals.

When all are thoroughly dried, pack petals into rose jar in layers; sprinkle each layer very lightly with salt.

When jar is filled, cork tightly; allow to stand 3 weeks.

Remove petals from jar and place in large mixing bowl. Blend orris root and all spices well; add to rose petals; add dried lemon verbena leaves. Return all to jar; cork tightly for 6 weeks.

When jar is ready for use, shake gently; uncover; drop oil of jasmine into jar. Exquisite fragrance fills the room.

Mother's Rose Jar Recipe   TIME: Variable

Rose petals   *¼ oz. allspice*
5 drops oil of rose geranium   *¼ oz. nutmeg*
5 drops glycerin   *¼ oz. cinnamon*
Pure grain alcohol   *¼ oz. powdered orris root*
Coarse salt   *1 oz. dried lavender flowers*
            ½ oz. dried heliotrope flowers

Gather fresh, unbruised rose petals every day after dew has evaporated but before the roses have lost their fragrance; separate petals carefully; spread on clean cloth or screen in shade for a day to dry partially.

Place oil of rose geranium and glycerin in rose jar; add layer of petals as each lot is dried; pour 1 teaspoon grain alcohol over each layer as it is added.

When jar (holding about 1 quart) is more than ¾ full, sprinkle lightly with coarse salt; cover tightly; shake every day for 2 weeks.

In mixing bowl, blend all spices with lavender and heliotrope; shake well; add to rose petals; shake again; cover tightly; allow to stand another week.

When ready for use, shake rose jar gently; uncover; add few drops grain alcohol. The room will be scented with the sweetness of a breath-taking fragrance.

If mixture is placed in small jars, care should be taken that some of the fixative and spices are in each jar.

Rose Petal Sachet Powder   TIME: *Variable*

4 ozs. dried rose petals   *10 drops oil of rose com-*
2 ozs. sandalwood, ground*   *pound**

Collect the velvety petals of excessively fragrant deep red roses; dry carefully on a cheesecloth-covered screen, or purchase dried petals from herb dealers.

Crush dried petals slightly; place in wooden bowl; blend

*May be purchased at some drugstores; also from herb dealers.

petals with ground sandalwood; fill jar with mixture; pour oil of rose compound over mixture; cover tightly; allow to stand at room temperature.

Shake occasionally; age 2 to 3 weeks.

Fill small muslin or taffeta sachet bags of desired shapes.

Use to scent lingerie.

Flower Petals Sachet Powder

1¾ cups mixed flower petals, powdered
¼ cup dried lemon verbena leaves, powdered
10 drops oil of rose geranium

Dry fragrant flower petals of one's choice. See Chapter Five, "Drying Herbs."

Crush and powder dried petals and lemon verbena leaves in mortar with pestle, or in wooden bowl.

Mix well; place in jar; add drops of rose geranium oil, which may be purchased at some drugstores and from herb dealers.

Shake occasionally; allow to age from 3 to 4 weeks.

Fill muslin or taffeta sachet bags of desired shapes and sizes.

Use as desired *to scent linens* and *lingerie.*

Lavender Sachet Solo   AGE: 2 to 3 weeks

4 ozs. dried lavender flowers   2 drops oil of lavender
¼ oz. powdered gum benzoin

Crush dried flowers until powdery; stir in powdered gum of benzoin; mix well.

Place mixture in jar; add oil of lavender drops; cover jar tightly; allow to stand at room temperature.

Shake mixture occasionally; age 2 to 3 weeks.

Fill small muslin or taffeta sachet bags of desired shapes.

Use *to scent clothes, linens,* and *lingerie.*

Portuguese Sachet Powder   AGE: 2 to 3 weeks

4 ozs. dried orange peel   2 drops oil of lemon grass
2 ozs. dried lemon peel   10 drops oil of orange flowers
2 ozs. orris root, powdered   20 drops oil of orange peel

Crush and powder dried orange and lemon peel in mortar with pestle or in wooden bowl.

Mix well with powdered orris root; place mixture in jar; add all drops of oil; cover jar tightly; allow to stand at room temperature.

Shake mixture occasionally; allow to age 2 to 3 weeks.

Fill small muslin or taffeta sachet bags of desired shapes.

Place among linens and *lingerie* as desired.

Rosemary Pillow of Remembrance   TIME: Variable

Half rosemary leaves and   Half pine needles
flowers

Select rosemary leaves and flowers which are newly dried and filled with fragrance. See Chapter Five, "Drying Herbs."

Pick fragrant pine needles; dry thoroughly before using.

In wooden bowl blend pine needles and rosemary leaves and flowers; crush slightly.

Fill muslin or taffeta bags of desired sizes and shapes with fragrant mixture. Slip bag into a decorative covering of thin material if desired.

Place rosemary bag or pillow under sleeping pillow, or use as sachet for linen closets and lingerie.

SUGGESTED ADDITIONAL COMBINATIONS:
    Lemon verbena and pine needles
    Rose geranium and pine needles
    Summer savory and pine needles

Sweet-Scented Bath Blend   TIME: Variable

Fresh rose geranium leaves,   1 qt. boiling water
about 4 tbs.

Pick leaves in early morning after all dew has evaporated. Wash them if necessary.

Crush or bruise leaves lightly; tie in a 4-inch square of soft muslin.

Infuse sachet bag in 1 qt. boiling water 15 minutes. Add scented water to bath.

To save time, sachet bag may be dropped directly into the bath without infusing.

NOTE: Any favorite fragrant herb such as *lavender, lemon verbena, mint, rosemary,* and *woodruff* may be prepared and used in the same way.

Clove Orange Pomanders   TIME: Variable

2 small oranges   *2 tsp. powdered orris root*
3 ozs. whole cloves

Select firm, thin-skinned, perfect fruit.

Spread cloves on wax paper or mixing board; use cloves with heads still on; save others to fill in vacant spots when making a pattern on fruit skins.

With large darning needle or pointed meat skewer pierce holes in skin of fruits; insert cloves, allowing heads to form pattern. Take care not to make a straight line, for this will cause the skin to split; neither hold the fruit too tightly for the same reason. Should a split occur, it will heal within a few days.

As the fruit dries, it will shrink; when completely cured, no part of the skin will show.

When fruit is completely filled with cloves, place carefully in a shallow bowl; sprinkle specific spice over fruit until well covered.

Place each coated fruit in a small separate square of cheese-cloth; tie carefully; suspend in warm, dry place; allow to dry from 3 to 6 weeks.

Use pomander to *perfume clothes* and *linen closets.* It will *protect clothing from moths.* Also allow several pomanders to stand in a bowl in a room. The aroma will fill the air with delightful fragrance.

To prepare other fruit pomanders:

APPLE POMANDER: Select small, firm red apples. Follow recipe; finally roll in ground cinnamon.
KUMQUAT or CHINESE QUINCE POMANDER. Select firm, perfect fruits. Follow recipe; finally roll in ground allspice.
LEMON POMANDER: Select firm, perfect fruits. Follow recipe; finally roll in ground cloves.
LIME POMANDER: Select firm, perfect fruits. Follow recipe; finally roll in ground nutmeg.

Sweet-Scented Lotions   INFUSE: 2 weeks

Leafy tops of lemon balm   *Rubbing alcohol*

Pick leafy tops in morning of hot day as soon as all dew has evaporated. If necessary, wash leaves carefully in cold running water. Dry on absorbent paper.

Crush leaves slightly using mortar and pestle. Fill pint jar ¼ full of crushed leaves; pour best-quality rubbing alcohol over leaves to within an inch of the top.

Cover jar tightly; allow to stand at room temperature 2 weeks, shaking occasionally.

Filter scented liquid through filter paper; bottle; cork tightly.
Use as rubbing alcohol.
Refreshing and stimulating.

NOTE: Any preferred fragrant herb leaves and flowering tops, such as *lavender, lemon verbena, rose geranium, rose petals, sweet marjoram,* and *thyme,* may be used to prepare scented rubbing lotion.

Sweet-Scented Moth Preventive No. 1

4 tbs. dried thyme   *1 tbs. ground cloves*
4 tbs. dried tansy   *4 tbs. dried southernwood**

In mixing bowl blend and crush dried herbs well.
Tie in small muslin bags about 4 or 5 inches square.
Hang sweet-scented bags among winter clothes.
Yield: 12 to 14 bags.

Sweet-Scented Moth Preventive No. 2

4 tbs. dried mint   *4 tbs. dried tansy*
4 tbs. santolina*   *4 tbs. wormwood**

In mixing bowl blend and crush dried herbs well.
Tie in small muslin bags about 4 inches square.
Hang sweet-scented bags among winter clothes.
Yield: 12 to 16 bags.

*May be purchased at drugstores; also from herb dealers.

CHAPTER ELEVEN

Fragrant Herbs
and Blossoms
Dried and Preserved
in Three Dimensions

This method of preserving herbs and flowers in their natural form and color was devised by Mrs. Frances R. Williams of Winchester, Massachusetts, more than twelve years ago. Mrs. Williams is a member of The New York Botanical Garden, The Brooklyn Botanical Garden, and of the Massachusetts Horticultural Society. She calls her work and hobby "drying plants in three dimensions."

Plants and blossoms dried in three dimensions are used for reference, study, and exhibitions. The herbs and flowers preserved by Mrs. Williams have been on exhibition in the library of The New York Botanical Garden, at Horticulture Hall in Boston, and at The Berkshire Garden Center in Stockbridge, Massachusetts, as well as at numerous regional exhibitions and meetings of The Herb Society of America.

UNIQUE METHOD

Like many an invention, the process of three-dimensional drying was developed as the result of ideas "clicking." At the time Mrs. Williams was pressing gardenias flat in alum for the permanent herbarium of The Herb Society of America at Horticulture Hall, she observed a plaster cast being prepared.

185

She realized that the plaster of paris was absorbing a great deal of the moisture. At that moment the idea of flowers dried in three dimensions suddenly occurred to her. She decided to experiment, little realizing what the lovely results would be. Simply taking a long chance, she covered one gardenia with plaster of paris and forgot about the little box for three weeks. Later, when she gently shook the blossom from the powder, to her amazement the gardenia was almost as perfect-looking as when it was fresh.

This surprising incident spurred her on to experiment further with various plants and different drying powders. One day a druggist suggested using ordinary household borax, which has proved to be a most satisfactory alkaline powder. Since those early days of experimenting Mrs. Williams has used many combinations of drying powders in order to test their effects upon various plants or upon the same plant. Separately, and in combinations, alum, plaster of paris, French chalk, baking soda, powdered sugar, fuller's earth, potato flour, orris-root powder, sand, talcum powder, whiting, and rice flour have been tried. Boric acid has been used as an acid powder for the acid plants. On others, attempts have been made to improve the results by the use of ordinary powdered chalk, cornstarch, dusting sulphur, naphtha flakes, elastic starch, and even bread flour. Some of the drying powders seem to add extra strength to the texture of the flowers, while others will change the natural colors of the blossoms. However, though Mrs. Williams has experimented with so many combinations, she recommends the use of plain household borax, and feels certain that one can achieve great success with the fragrant garden herbs for exhibition purposes.

Successes and failures: Through the years of experimenting Mrs. Williams has kept an accurate record of more than 150 species of the flowers and herbs of New England with which she has worked. She has a complete list of what she calls her "successes and failures." A *success* to her means that the dried appearance is like that of the fresh flower; that the color and shape are good; and that the dried specimens are still beautiful to look upon even six and eight years later.

Many herbs have been dried in borax. As Mrs. Williams has observed the preservation of the plants over the years, her mind has been working on the idea of discovering a way to make the dried flowers softer and more pliable. In present experimenting talcum powder or boric acid powder, or a combination of talcum powder and plaster of paris are being used. So far the results which really please her have not been achieved.

If the plants need to be stored for any length of time they are given an extra sprinkling of borax, and moth balls are put into the box. This combination acts as an insecticide and keeps the carpet beetles away. The three-dimensional herbs and blossoms retain their natural forms better when not covered with tissue paper, for the weight has a tendency to flatten the blossoms.

The clear vivid pinks and the shades of pure yellow blossoms hold their colors the most perfectly. The shades of blue will vary from the natural fresh color, and the reds have completely and consistently eluded and defied experimentation. The rich red hues will turn into shades of sand and pink or will drop all brilliance and reflect only a dull, lifeless shade. The pure whites, after more than three years, may reflect an oyster white, but after that they turn to a light brown. The blues of the "Heavenly Blue" morning-glory will revert to bright and vivid pinks.

BOUQUETS OF DRIED HERBS IN THREE DIMENSIONS

The method of drying herbs and flowers in their three dimensions of pure naturalness requires a real love of beauty combined with great patience and a goodly supply of borax. Those culinary, fragrant herbs which have proved successful are listed at the end of these paragraphs. Mrs. Williams also suggests drying small flowers to be used for decorating tiny gift boxes of dried lavender blossoms and other potpourris. Combinations of dried three-dimensional herbs make charming bouquets.

The amount of drying powder necessary depends upon the size of the plant and of the box in which it is placed. When a small shoe box is large enough to hold the herbs or flowers which are to be preserved, two or three pounds of borax will be sufficient. However, if one is working with three or four long pieces of angelica, as much as twenty pounds of borax may be needed to cover the herb.

PROCEDURE FOR THREE DIMENSIONAL
DRYING AND PRESERVING

Select the most perfect specimen at the time when the herb is
just beginning to be in full blossom.

Cut the herb when it and the blossoms are completely fresh,
free of all dew, moisture, dust, and faded leaves.

Select a box or carton slightly longer than the herb and 2 inches
higher or deeper. A carton which unfolds at the corners is
helpful when removing the borax.

When drying a large specimen, insert into the carton a wire tray
made of poultry wire, which may be easily lifted from the
carton.

Cover bottom of carton with borax or selected drying powder
to the depth of ½ inch.

Pour into the carton a mound of powder high enough for the
blossom to rest in its natural form. The flower or blossom
should not lie down.

With deft, light fingers or a very small spoon, carefully pour
powder *under the blossom.*

When blossom is slightly more than half covered, sprinkle
powder lightly into the blossom.

Slowly continue to pour in powder to bank the blossom completely underneath.

Fill in all spaces from every side.

Gently cover the entire herb to the depth of ½ inch over the
top.

Never throw the powder over the herb carelessly or too fast,
or the blossoms and the leaves will be flattened.

Allow uncovered carton to stand in room at ordinary room
temperature for 3 weeks. *Do not place near heat,* for this
may make the plant too brittle. Naturally moist plants and
flowers such as mushrooms and skunk cabbage require 6
weeks or more for three-dimensional drying.

Never shake or jar the carton, for all motion tends to flatten
the leaves.

When drying time has elapsed, gradually lift up the tray to
allow powder to sift out.

To remove the herb from the tray, use great care and gentle-
ness.

Remove any clinging powder by gently shaking the herb, or by gently tapping the stem with a pencil, or by brushing with a very soft brush.

Keep a complete record of your success with each herb.

If herbs need to be stored for any length of time, place them in a box, add moth balls. Do not cover the herbs with tissue paper. Cover box or carton only.

If three-dimensional herbs are mailed, fasten stems gently to bottom of carton with one or two stitches, or place the specimen in a box into which it fits snugly. A lightweight facial tissue may be used to cover the specimen.

It is said that herbs and flowers dried and preserved by this three-dimensional method would retain their natural colors for 50 years if they were kept at Pikes Peak. In the high, dry altitude the specimens would not deteriorate. However, at sea level the average number of years during which the three-dimensional specimens retain their natural colors and forms is from 5 to 6 years.

FRAGRANT HERBS WHICH RETAIN THEIR NATURAL BEAUTY WHEN DRIED IN THREE DIMENSIONS

Herbs with blossoms

Basil, Sweet, *Ocimum basilicum*

Bergamot Mint, *Mentha piperita,* var. *citrata*
or
Orange Mint, *Mentha piperita,* var. *citrata*

Chervil, *Anthriscus cerefolium*

Chives, *Allium schoenoprasum*

Coriander, *Coriandrum sativum*

Costmary, *Chrysanthemum balsamita*

Dill, *Anethum graveolens*

Fennel, Sweet, *Foeniculum vulgare,* var. *dulce*

Lovage, *Levisticum officinale*

Marjoram, Wild, *Origanum vulgare*

Peppermint, *Mentha piperita*

Sage, *Salvia officinalis*

Savory, Summer, *Satureia hortensis*

Spearmint, *Mentha spicata*
Tansy, *Tanacetum vulgare*
Thyme, *Thymus vulgaris*

Herb leaves

Burnet, *Sanguisorba minor*
Lovage, *Levisticum officinale*
Rosemary, *Rosmarinus officinalis*
Sage, *Salvia officinalis*
Tarragon, *Artemisia dracunculus*

Glossary

BOTANICAL NAMES OF HERBS AND SPICES INCLUDED IN THIS VOLUME

Allium Amelophrasum	Leek, wild in Europe
Allium Ascalonicum	Shallot
Allium Cepa	Onion
Allium Porrum	Leek, cultivated
Allium Sativum	Garlic
Allium Schoenoprasum	Chives
Allium Tricoccum	Leek, wild in America
Alpinia Galanga	Galangal
Angelica Archangelica Officinalis	Angelica
Angelica Atropurpurea	Angelica, popular American species
Anethum Graveolens	Dill
Anthemis Nobilis	Camomile, English or Roman
Anthriscus Cerefolium	Chervil
Apium Graveolens	Celery
Artemisia Dracunculus	Tarragon, French
Asperula Odorata	Woodruff, Sweet
Barbarea Verna	Cress, Belle Isle
Borago Officinalis	Borage
Brassica Sinapis	Mustard Plant
Brassica Sinapis Alba	Mustard, White
Brassica Sinapis Nigra	Mustard, Black

191

Calendula Officinalis	Marigold
Capsicum Annuum Linn	Pepper, Red, Paprika
Capsicum Baccatum Linn	Pepper, Red, Cayenne
Capsicum Frutescens Linn	Pepper, Red, Cayenne
Carthamus Tinctorius L.	Safflower
Carum Carvi	Caraway
Caryophyllus Aromaticus L.	Clove
Chile Ancho, var. *Acuminatum*	Chili, Mexican
Chrysanthemum Balsamita	Costmary
Cinnamomum Burmanni Blume	Cassia, Batavia
Cinnamomum Cassia Blume	Bark, Chinese Cinnamon
Cinnamomum Loureirii Nees	Cinnamon, French Indo-China
Cinnamomum Zeylanicum Nees	Cinnamon, True
Coriandrum Sativum	Coriander
Crocus Sativus	Saffron
Cuminum Cyminum	Cumin or *Comino*
Curcuma Longa L.	Turmeric
Curcuma Zedoaria	Zedoary
Foeniculum Vulgare	Fennel, Wild
Foeniculum Vulgare, var. *Dulce*	Fennel, Sweet, or Florence
Hyssopus Alba	Hyssop, White
Hyssopus Officinalis	Hyssop
Hyssopus Rubra	Hyssop, Pink
Illicium Verum	Anise Seed, Badian, Chinese, Star
Juniperus Communis	Juniper, Wild
Laurus Nobilis	Bay, Sweet, or Laurel
Lavandula Spica	Lavender, Spike
Lavandula Stoechas	Lavender, French
Lavandula Vera	Lavender, English or True
Lepidium Sativum	Cress, Land
Levisticum Officinale	Lovage
Lippia Citriodora	Verbena, Lemon

Marrubium Vulgare	Horehound
Matricaria Chamomilla	Camomile, German or Hungarian
Melissa Officinalis	Balm, Lemon
Mentha Citrata	Mint, Orange
Mentha Gentilis Variegata	Mint, American Apple
Mentha Piperita	Peppermint
Mentha Piperita, var. *Officinalis*	Peppermint, White
Mentha Piperita, var. *Vulgaris*	Peppermint, Black
Mentha Rotundifolia	Mint, Apple
Mentha Spicata	Spearmint
Mentha Spicata, var. *Crispata*	Mint, Curly
Monarda Citriodora	Bergamot, Lemon
Monarda Didyma	Bergamot, Red
Monarda Fistulosa	Bergamot, or Wild Bergamot
Myristica Agentiea Warb.	Mace, Papua, Macassar
Myristica Fragrans Houtt	Mace; also Nutmeg
Myristica Malabrica Lam.	Mace, Bombay, or Wild
Nepeta Cataria	Catnip
Nigella Sativa	Cumin, Black
Ocimum Basilicum	Basil, Sweet
Ocimum Basilicum Sanctum	Basil, Holy
Ocimum Citriodora	Basil, Lemon
Ocimum Crispum	Basil, Italian or Curly
Ocimum Minimum	Basil, Dwarf; Green or Purple
Origanum Marjorana L.	Marjoram, Sweet
Origanum Onites	Marjoram, Pot
Origanum Vulgare	Marjoram, Wild
Papaver Rhoeas	Poppy
Papaver Somniferum	Poppy, Opium
Pelargonium Capitalum	Rose Geranium
Pelargonium Graveolens	Rose Geranium
Petroselinum Hortense	Parsley
Petroselinum Hortense, var. *Crispum*	Parsley, Curly
Petroselinum Hortense, var. *Filicinum*	Parsley, Fern-leaved

Pimenta Karst	Allspice
Pimenta Officinalis L.	Allspice
Pimpinella Anisum	Anise
Pimpinella Saxifraga L.	Burnet, European
Piper Nigrum L.	Pepper, Black
Radicula Armoracia	Horseradish
Rorippa Armoracia	Horseradish
Rosa Damascena	Rose, Damask
Rosa Gallica	Rose de Provins
Rosa Chinensis	Rose, China
Rosmarinus Officinalis	Rosemary
Rumex Acetosa	Sorrel, Garden
Rumex Scutatus	Sorrel, French
Ruta Graveolens	Rue
Salvia Horminum	Sage, Garden, or Horminum
Salvia Officinalis	Sage, Garden
Salvia Officinalis Alba	Sage, White
Salvia Pratensis	Sage, Meadow
Salvia Sclarea	Sage, Clary
Salvia Splendens	Sage, Pineapple
Sanguisorba Minor	Burnet, Salad
Sanguisorba Officinalis	Burnet, Great
Satureia Hortensis	Savory, Summer
Satureia Montana	Savory, Winter
Sesamum Indicum	Sesame
Sesamum Orientale	Sesame or Bene
Sisymbrium Nasturtium Aquaticum	Water Cress
Tanacetum Vulgare	Tansy, Common
Tanacetum Vulgare, var. Crispum	Tansy, Fern-leaved
Thymus Serpyllum	Thyme, Wild
Thymus Serpyllum Albus	Thyme, White
Thymus Serpyllum Cocineus	Thyme, Trailing Scarlet
Thymus Serpyllum Lanuginosus	Thyme, Woolly
Thymus Serpyllum, var. Citriodorus	Thyme, Lemon
Thymus Vulgaris	Thyme, English or Garden
Tropaeolum Majus	Nasturtium

Umbellularia Californica	Bay or Laurel, California
Valerianella Lacustra	Corn Salad
Verbena Hastata	Vervain, American
Verbena Officinalis	Vervain, European
Zingiber Officinale Roscoe	Ginger

BOTANICAL FAMILY NAMES OF HERBS AND SPICES INCLUDED IN THIS VOLUME

Asteraceae
   Marigold

Boraginaceae
   Borage

Brassicaceae
   Cress, Land
   Cress, Water
   Horseradish

Compositae
   Camomile, German
   Camomile, Roman
   Costmary
   Safflower or
   Saffron, Mexican
   Tansy, Common
   Tansy, Fernleaf
   Tarragon, French

Cruciferae
   Mustard, Black
   Mustard, White

Geraniaceae
   Rose Geranium

Iridaceae
   Saffron, True

Labiatae
   Balm, Lemon
   Basil, Dwarf
   Basil, Italian or Curly
   Basil, Lemon
   Basil, Sweet
   Bergamot
   Catnip
   Horehound
   Hyssop
   Lavender, French
   Lavender, Spike
   Lavender, True or English
   Marjoram, Pot
   Marjoram, Sweet
   Marjoram, Wild
   Mint, Apple
   Mint, Apple, American
   Mint, Curly
   Mint, Orange
   Orégano
   Peppermint, Black
   Peppermint, White
   Rosemary
   Sage, Clary
   Sage, Garden
   Sage, Pineapple
   Sage, White
   Salvia Horminum
   Savory, Summer

Savory, Winter
Spearmint
Thyme, English or
    Garden
Thyme, Lemon
Thyme, Wild
Thyme, Woolly

Lauraceae
Bay, Sweet
Cassia
Cinnamon

Liliaceae
Chives
Garlic
Leek
Onion
Shallot

Myristicaeae
Mace
Nutmeg

Myrtaceae
Allspice
Cloves

Papaveraceae

Poppy, Dutch
Pedaliaceae
Sesame

Pinaceae
Juniper Berries

Piperaceae
Pepper, Black
Pepper, White

Polygonaceae
Sorrel, French
Sorrel, Garden

Sorrel, Mountain
Sorrel, Silver Le

Rosaceae
Burnet, Great
Burnet, Salad
Burnet, Wild
Rose

Rubiaceae
Woodruff, Sweet

Rutaceae
Rue

Solanaceae
Peppers, Chili, Mexican
Louisiana Sport

Tropaeolaceae
Nasturtium, Dwarf
Nasturtium, Wild

Umbelliferae
Angelica, American
Angelica, Garden
Anise, Jamaica
Caraway
Celery
Chervil
Coriander
Cumin, or *Comino*
Cumin, Black
Dill
Fennel, Common, or Wild
Fennel, Dwarf, or *Finocchio*
Fennel, Florence
Fennel, Sweet, or *Carosella*
Lovage, or Love Parsley
Lovage, Scottish, or Sea
Lovage, Wild
Parsley, Double-curled
Parsley, Fern-leaved

Valerianaceae
    Corn Salad

Verbenaceae
    Verbena, Lemon

Zingiberaceae
    Cardamom
    Ginger, Dried, Black
    Ginger, Dried, Green
    Ginger, Dried, Peeled
    Ginger, Florida
    Ginger, Jamaica
    Turmeric

Index

200   *Index*

NASTOIKA, 157. *See also* Ginger
NASTURTIUM, 32, 107–8, 194, 196
  Characteristics, 108
  Cultivating, 108
  Dwarf, 196
  Harvesting, 108
  History, 107–8
  Uses, Leaves, 108
    Seed, 108
Nepeta cataria, 73, 193
New York Pepper Exchange, The, 164
Nigella sativa, 83, 193
NUTMEG, 160–62, 193, 196. *See also* Mace (or True Mace)
  Characteristics, Groves, 161
    Seed, 160, 162
    Spice, 160–61
    Trees, 161
  Connecticut, State of, 162
  Cultivated, How, 162
  Gai gai, 162
  Harvested, How, 162
  History, 161–62
  in Pomander, Lime, 182
  in Potpourri, Rose(s), 178
  in Rose Jar, 179
  in Sachets, 175
  Legendry, 161–62
  Penang, 161
  Production, Commercial, 161
  Sketch by Aldo Becci, *end papers*
  Uses, 162
NUTMEG-GERANIUM, 119. *See also* Rose Geranium
Nutmeg State, the, 162

Ocimum basilicum, 61, 63, 193
Ocimum basilicum sanctum, 62, 193
Ocimum citriodora, 63, 193
Ocimum crispum, 62, 193
Ocimum minimum, 62, 193

Old-Fashioned Recipe for Herb Butter, 55
Olde Thompson Pepper Mills, 165
ONION, 108–10, 191, 196. *See also* Chives; Garlic; Leek; Shallot
  Bermuda, 109
  Characteristics, 108–9
  Creole, Red, 109
    White, 109
  Cultivating, 109–10
  Globe, Portugal, White, 109
    Southport, Red, 109
    Yellow, 109
  Harvesting, Mature, 110
    Scallions, 110
  History, 108
  Powder, 109
  Prizetaker, 109
  Salt, 109
  Scallions, 109, 110
  Spanish, 109
  Uses, 109
OPIUM POPPY, 114, 193. *See also* Poppy Seed
ORANGE-GERANIUM, 119. *See also* Rose Geranium
ORANGE MINT, 103, 104, 189, 195. *See also* Mint(s)
Orange Pomander, 182
ORÉGANO, 25, 27, 28, 41, 42, 43, 44, 110–11. *See also* Marjoram (or Sweet Marjoram)
  Characteristics, 110
  Cultivating, 111
  Harvesting, 111
  Uses, Leaves, 110–11
    Powdered, 111
Orientals, the, 62, 73, 74, 77, 78, 87, 96, 108, 129, 154, 157
Origanum marjorana, L., 100, 101, 193
Origanum onites, 101, 193

A CATALOG OF SELECTED
DOVER BOOKS
IN ALL FIELDS OF INTEREST

A CATALOG OF SELECTED DOVER
BOOKS IN ALL FIELDS OF INTEREST

DRAWINGS OF REMBRANDT, edited by Seymour Slive. Updated Lippmann, Hofstede de Groot edition, with definitive scholarly apparatus. All portraits, biblical sketches, landscapes, nudes. Oriental figures, classical studies, together with selection of work by followers. 550 illustrations. Total of 630pp. 9⅛ × 12¼.
21485-0, 21486-9 Pa., Two-vol. set $25.00

GHOST AND HORROR STORIES OF AMBROSE BIERCE, Ambrose Bierce. 24 tales vividly imagined, strangely prophetic, and decades ahead of their time in technical skill: "The Damned Thing," "An Inhabitant of Carcosa," "The Eyes of the Panther," "Moxon's Master," and 20 more. 199pp. 5⅜ × 8½. 20767-6 Pa. $3.95

ETHICAL WRITINGS OF MAIMONIDES, Maimonides. Most significant ethical works of great medieval sage, newly translated for utmost precision, readability. Laws Concerning Character Traits, Eight Chapters, more. 192pp. 5⅜ × 8½.
24522-5 Pa. $4.50

THE EXPLORATION OF THE COLORADO RIVER AND ITS CANYONS, J. W. Powell. Full text of Powell's 1,000-mile expedition down the fabled Colorado in 1869. Superb account of terrain, geology, vegetation, Indians, famine, mutiny, treacherous rapids, mighty canyons, during exploration of last unknown part of continental U.S. 400pp. 5⅜ × 8½. 20094-9 Pa. $6.95

HISTORY OF PHILOSOPHY, Julián Marías. Clearest one-volume history on the market. Every major philosopher and dozens of others, to Existentialism and later. 505pp. 5⅜ × 8½. 21739-6 Pa. $8.50

ALL ABOUT LIGHTNING, Martin A. Uman. Highly readable non-technical survey of nature and causes of lightning, thunderstorms, ball lightning, St. Elmo's Fire, much more. Illustrated. 192pp. 5⅜ × 8½. 25237-X Pa. $5.95

SAILING ALONE AROUND THE WORLD, Captain Joshua Slocum. First man to sail around the world, alone, in small boat. One of great feats of seamanship told in delightful manner. 67 illustrations. 294pp. 5⅜ × 8½. 20326-3 Pa. $4.50

LETTERS AND NOTES ON THE MANNERS, CUSTOMS AND CONDITIONS OF THE NORTH AMERICAN INDIANS, George Catlin. Classic account of life among Plains Indians: ceremonies, hunt, warfare, etc. 312 plates. 572pp. of text. 6⅛ × 9¼. 22118-0, 22119-9 Pa. Two-vol. set $15.90

ALASKA: The Harriman Expedition, 1899, John Burroughs, John Muir, et al. Informative, engrossing accounts of two-month, 9,000-mile expedition. Native peoples, wildlife, forests, geography, salmon industry, glaciers, more. Profusely illustrated. 240 black-and-white line drawings. 124 black-and-white photographs. 3 maps. Index. 576pp. 5⅜ × 8½. 25109-8 Pa. $11.95

HOW TO WRITE, Gertrude Stein. Gertrude Stein claimed anyone could understand her unconventional writing—here are clues to help. Fascinating improvisations, language experiments, explanations illuminate Stein's craft and the art of writing. Total of 414pp. 4⅝ × 6⅜. 23144-5 Pa. $5.95

ADVENTURES AT SEA IN THE GREAT AGE OF SAIL: Five Firsthand Narratives, edited by Elliot Snow. Rare true accounts of exploration, whaling, shipwreck, fierce natives, trade, shipboard life, more. 33 illustrations. Introduction. 353pp. 5⅜ × 8½. 25177-2 Pa. $7.95

THE HERBAL OR GENERAL HISTORY OF PLANTS, John Gerard. Classic descriptions of about 2,850 plants—with over 2,700 illustrations—includes Latin and English names, physical descriptions, varieties, time and place of growth, more. 2,706 illustrations. xlv + 1,678pp. 8½ × 12¼. 23147-X Cloth. $75.00

DOROTHY AND THE WIZARD IN OZ, L. Frank Baum. Dorothy and the Wizard visit the center of the Earth, where people are vegetables, glass houses grow and Oz characters reappear. Classic sequel to *Wizard of Oz*. 256pp. 5⅜ × 8. 24714-7 Pa. $4.95

SONGS OF EXPERIENCE: Facsimile Reproduction with 26 Plates in Full Color, William Blake. This facsimile of Blake's original "Illuminated Book" reproduces 26 full-color plates from a rare 1826 edition. Includes "The Tyger," "London," "Holy Thursday," and other immortal poems. 26 color plates. Printed text of poems. 48pp. 5¼ × 7. 24636-1 Pa. $3.50

SONGS OF INNOCENCE, William Blake. The first and most popular of Blake's famous "Illuminated Books," in a facsimile edition reproducing all 31 brightly colored plates. Additional printed text of each poem. 64pp. 5¼ × 7. 22764-2 Pa. $3.50

PRECIOUS STONES, Max Bauer. Classic, thorough study of diamonds, rubies, emeralds, garnets, etc.: physical character, occurrence, properties, use, similar topics. 20 plates, 8 in color. 94 figures. 659pp. 6⅛ × 9¼. 21910-0, 21911-9 Pa., Two-vol. set $14.90

ENCYCLOPEDIA OF VICTORIAN NEEDLEWORK, S. F. A. Caulfeild and Blanche Saward. Full, precise descriptions of stitches, techniques for dozens of needlecrafts—most exhaustive reference of its kind. Over 800 figures. Total of 679pp. 8⅛ × 11. Two volumes. Vol. 1 22800-2 Pa. $10.95
Vol. 2 22801-0 Pa. $10.95

THE MARVELOUS LAND OF OZ, L. Frank Baum. Second Oz book, the Scarecrow and Tin Woodman are back with hero named Tip, Oz magic. 136 illustrations. 287pp. 5⅜ × 8½. 20692-0 Pa. $5.95

WILD FOWL DECOYS, Joel Barber. Basic book on the subject, by foremost authority and collector. Reveals history of decoy making and rigging, place in American culture, different kinds of decoys, how to make them, and how to use them. 140 plates. 156pp. 7⅞ × 10¾. 20011-6 Pa. $7.95

HISTORY OF LACE, Mrs. Bury Palliser. Definitive, profusely illustrated chronicle of lace from earliest times to late 19th century. Laces of Italy, Greece, England, France, Belgium, etc. Landmark of needlework scholarship. 266 illustrations. 672pp. 6⅛ × 9¼. 24742-2 Pa. $14.95

ILLUSTRATED GUIDE TO SHAKER FURNITURE, Robert Meader. All furniture and appurtenances, with much on unknown local styles. 235 photos. 146pp. 9 × 12. 22819-3 Pa. $7.95

WHALE SHIPS AND WHALING: A Pictorial Survey, George Francis Dow. Over 200 vintage engravings, drawings, photographs of barks, brigs, cutters, other vessels. Also harpoons, lances, whaling guns, many other artifacts. Comprehensive text by foremost authority. 207 black-and-white illustrations. 288pp. 6 × 9. 24808-9 Pa. $8.95

THE BERTRAMS, Anthony Trollope. Powerful portrayal of blind self-will and thwarted ambition includes one of Trollope's most heartrending love stories. 497pp. 5⅜ × 8½. 25119-5 Pa. $8.95

ADVENTURES WITH A HAND LENS, Richard Headstrom. Clearly written guide to observing and studying flowers and grasses, fish scales, moth and insect wings, egg cases, buds, feathers, seeds, leaf scars, moss, molds, ferns, common crystals, etc.—all with an ordinary, inexpensive magnifying glass. 209 exact line drawings aid in your discoveries. 220pp. 5⅜ × 8½. 23330-8 Pa. $3.95

RODIN ON ART AND ARTISTS, Auguste Rodin. Great sculptor's candid, wide-ranging comments on meaning of art; great artists; relation of sculpture to poetry, painting, music; philosophy of life, more. 76 superb black-and-white illustrations of Rodin's sculpture, drawings and prints. 119pp. 8⅜ × 11¼. 24487-3 Pa. $6.95

FIFTY CLASSIC FRENCH FILMS, 1912–1982: A Pictorial Record, Anthony Slide. Memorable stills from Grand Illusion, Beauty and the Beast, Hiroshima, Mon Amour, many more. Credits, plot synopses, reviews, etc. 160pp. 8¼ × 11. 25256-6 Pa. $11.95

THE PRINCIPLES OF PSYCHOLOGY, William James. Famous long course complete, unabridged. Stream of thought, time perception, memory, experimental methods; great work decades ahead of its time. 94 figures. 1,391pp. 5⅜ × 8½. 20381-6, 20382-4 Pa., Two-vol. set $19.90

BODIES IN A BOOKSHOP, R. T. Campbell. Challenging mystery of blackmail and murder with ingenious plot and superbly drawn characters. In the best tradition of British suspense fiction. 192pp. 5⅜ × 8½. 24720-1 Pa. $3.95

CALLAS: PORTRAIT OF A PRIMA DONNA, George Jellinek. Renowned commentator on the musical scene chronicles incredible career and life of the most controversial, fascinating, influential operatic personality of our time. 64 black-and-white photographs. 416pp. 5⅜ × 8¼. 25047-4 Pa. $7.95

GEOMETRY, RELATIVITY AND THE FOURTH DIMENSION, Rudolph Rucker. Exposition of fourth dimension, concepts of relativity as Flatland characters continue adventures. Popular, easily followed yet accurate, profound. 141 illustrations. 133pp. 5⅜ × 8½. 23400-2 Pa. $3.50

HOUSEHOLD STORIES BY THE BROTHERS GRIMM, with pictures by Walter Crane. 53 classic stories—Rumpelstiltskin, Rapunzel, Hansel and Gretel, the Fisherman and his Wife, Snow White, Tom Thumb, Sleeping Beauty, Cinderella, and so much more—lavishly illustrated with original 19th century drawings. 114 illustrations. x + 269pp. 5⅜ × 8½. 21080-4 Pa. $4.50

SUNDIALS, Albert Waugh. Far and away the best, most thorough coverage of ideas, mathematics concerned, types, construction, adjusting anywhere. Over 100 illustrations. 230pp. 5⅜ × 8½. 22947-5 Pa. $4.00

PICTURE HISTORY OF THE NORMANDIE: With 190 Illustrations, Frank O. Braynard. Full story of legendary French ocean liner: Art Deco interiors, design innovations, furnishings, celebrities, maiden voyage, tragic fire, much more. Extensive text. 144pp. 8⅞ × 11¾. 25257-4 Pa. $9.95

THE FIRST AMERICAN COOKBOOK: A Facsimile of "American Cookery," 1796, Amelia Simmons. Facsimile of the first American-written cookbook published in the United States contains authentic recipes for colonial favorites—pumpkin pudding, winter squash pudding, spruce beer, Indian slapjacks, and more. Introductory Essay and Glossary of colonial cooking terms. 80pp. 5⅜ × 8½. 24710-4 Pa. $3.50

101 PUZZLES IN THOUGHT AND LOGIC, C. R. Wylie, Jr. Solve murders and robberies, find out which fishermen are liars, how a blind man could possibly identify a color—purely by your own reasoning! 107pp. 5⅜ × 8½. 20367-0 Pa. $2.00

THE BOOK OF WORLD-FAMOUS MUSIC—CLASSICAL, POPULAR AND FOLK, James J. Fuld. Revised and enlarged republication of landmark work in musico-bibliography. Full information about nearly 1,000 songs and compositions including first lines of music and lyrics. New supplement. Index. 800pp. 5⅜ × 8¼. 24857-7 Pa. $14.95

ANTHROPOLOGY AND MODERN LIFE, Franz Boas. Great anthropologist's classic treatise on race and culture. Introduction by Ruth Bunzel. Only inexpensive paperback edition. 255pp. 5⅜ × 8½. 25245-0 Pa. $5.95

THE TALE OF PETER RABBIT, Beatrix Potter. The inimitable Peter's terrifying adventure in Mr. McGregor's garden, with all 27 wonderful, full-color Potter illustrations. 55pp. 4¼ × 5½. (Available in U.S. only) 22827-4 Pa. $1.75

THREE PROPHETIC SCIENCE FICTION NOVELS, H. G. Wells. *When the Sleeper Wakes, A Story of the Days to Come* and *The Time Machine* (full version). 335pp. 5⅜ × 8½. (Available in U.S. only) 20605-X Pa. $5.95

APICIUS COOKERY AND DINING IN IMPERIAL ROME, edited and translated by Joseph Dommers Vehling. Oldest known cookbook in existence offers readers a clear picture of what foods Romans ate, how they prepared them, etc. 49 illustrations. 301pp. 6⅛ × 9¼. 23563-7 Pa. $6.00

SHAKESPEARE LEXICON AND QUOTATION DICTIONARY, Alexander Schmidt. Full definitions, locations, shades of meaning of every word in plays and poems. More than 50,000 exact quotations. 1,485pp. 6½ × 9¼. 22726-X, 22727-8 Pa., Two-vol. set $27.90

THE WORLD'S GREAT SPEECHES, edited by Lewis Copeland and Lawrence W. Lamm. Vast collection of 278 speeches from Greeks to 1970. Powerful and effective models; unique look at history. 842pp. 5⅜ × 8½. 20468-5 Pa. $10.95

THE BLUE FAIRY BOOK, Andrew Lang. The first, most famous collection, with many familiar tales: Little Red Riding Hood, Aladdin and the Wonderful Lamp, Puss in Boots, Sleeping Beauty, Hansel and Gretel, Rumpelstiltskin; 37 in all. 138 illustrations. 390pp. 5⅜ × 8½. 21437-0 Pa. $5.95

THE STORY OF THE CHAMPIONS OF THE ROUND TABLE, Howard Pyle. Sir Launcelot, Sir Tristram and Sir Percival in spirited adventures of love and triumph retold in Pyle's inimitable style. 50 drawings, 31 full-page. xviii + 329pp. 6½ × 9¼. 21883-X Pa. $6.95

AUDUBON AND HIS JOURNALS, Maria Audubon. Unmatched two-volume portrait of the great artist, naturalist and author contains his journals, an excellent biography by his granddaughter, expert annotations by the noted ornithologist, Dr. Elliott Coues, and 37 superb illustrations. Total of 1,200pp. 5⅜ × 8.
Vol. I 25143-8 Pa. $8.95
Vol. II 25144-6 Pa. $8.95

GREAT DINOSAUR HUNTERS AND THEIR DISCOVERIES, Edwin H. Colbert. Fascinating, lavishly illustrated chronicle of dinosaur research, 1820's to 1960. Achievements of Cope, Marsh, Brown, Buckland, Mantell, Huxley, many others. 384pp. 5¼ × 8¼. 24701-5 Pa. $6.95

THE TASTEMAKERS, Russell Lynes. Informal, illustrated social history of American taste 1850's–1950's. First popularized categories Highbrow, Lowbrow, Middlebrow. 129 illustrations. New (1979) afterword. 384pp. 6 × 9.
23993-4 Pa. $6.95

DOUBLE CROSS PURPOSES, Ronald A. Knox. A treasure hunt in the Scottish Highlands, an old map, unidentified corpse, surprise discoveries keep reader guessing in this cleverly intricate tale of financial skullduggery. 2 black-and-white maps. 320pp. 5⅜ × 8½. (Available in U.S. only) 25032-6 Pa. $5.95

AUTHENTIC VICTORIAN DECORATION AND ORNAMENTATION IN FULL COLOR: 46 Plates from "Studies in Design," Christopher Dresser. Superb full-color lithographs reproduced from rare original portfolio of a major Victorian designer. 48pp. 9¼ × 12¼. 25083-0 Pa. $7.95

PRIMITIVE ART, Franz Boas. Remains the best text ever prepared on subject, thoroughly discussing Indian, African, Asian, Australian, and, especially, Northern American primitive art. Over 950 illustrations show ceramics, masks, totem poles, weapons, textiles, paintings, much more. 376pp. 5⅜ × 8. 20025-6 Pa. $6.95

SIDELIGHTS ON RELATIVITY, Albert Einstein. Unabridged republication of two lectures delivered by the great physicist in 1920–21. *Ether and Relativity* and *Geometry and Experience*. Elegant ideas in non-mathematical form, accessible to intelligent layman. vi + 56pp. 5⅜ × 8½. 24511-X Pa. $2.95

THE WIT AND HUMOR OF OSCAR WILDE, edited by Alvin Redman. More than 1,000 ripostes, paradoxes, wisecracks: Work is the curse of the drinking classes, I can resist everything except temptation, etc. 258pp. 5⅜ × 8½. 20602-5 Pa. $3.95

ADVENTURES WITH A MICROSCOPE, Richard Headstrom. 59 adventures with clothing fibers, protozoa, ferns and lichens, roots and leaves, much more. 142 illustrations. 232pp. 5⅜ × 8½. 23471-1 Pa. $3.95

CATALOG OF DOVER BOOKS

PLANTS OF THE BIBLE, Harold N. Moldenke and Alma L. Moldenke. Standard reference to all 230 plants mentioned in Scriptures. Latin name, biblical reference, uses, modern identity, much more. Unsurpassed encyclopedic resource for scholars, botanists, nature lovers, students of Bible. Bibliography. Indexes. 123 black-and-white illustrations. 384pp. 6 × 9. 25069-5 Pa. $8.95

FAMOUS AMERICAN WOMEN: A Biographical Dictionary from Colonial Times to the Present, Robert McHenry, ed. From Pocahontas to Rosa Parks, 1,035 distinguished American women documented in separate biographical entries. Accurate, up-to-date data, numerous categories, spans 400 years. Indices. 493pp. 6½ × 9¼. 24523-3 Pa. $9.95

THE FABULOUS INTERIORS OF THE GREAT OCEAN LINERS IN HISTORIC PHOTOGRAPHS, William H. Miller, Jr. Some 200 superb photographs capture exquisite interiors of world's great "floating palaces"—1890's to 1980's: *Titanic, Ile de France, Queen Elizabeth, United States, Europa,* more. Approx. 200 black-and-white photographs. Captions. Text. Introduction. 160pp. 8⅜ × 11¼. 24756-2 Pa. $9.95

THE GREAT LUXURY LINERS, 1927-1954: A Photographic Record, William H. Miller, Jr. Nostalgic tribute to heyday of ocean liners. 186 photos of Ile de France, Normandie, Leviathan, Queen Elizabeth, United States, many others. Interior and exterior views. Introduction. Captions. 160pp. 9 × 12. 24056-8 Pa. $9.95

A NATURAL HISTORY OF THE DUCKS, John Charles Phillips. Great landmark of ornithology offers complete detailed coverage of nearly 200 species and subspecies of ducks: gadwall, sheldrake, merganser, pintail, many more. 74 full-color plates, 102 black-and-white. Bibliography. Total of 1,920pp. 8⅜ × 11¼. 25141-1, 25142-X Cloth. Two-vol. set $100.00

THE SEAWEED HANDBOOK: An Illustrated Guide to Seaweeds from North Carolina to Canada, Thomas F. Lee. Concise reference covers 78 species. Scientific and common names, habitat, distribution, more. Finding keys for easy identification. 224pp. 5⅜ × 8½. 25215-9 Pa. $5.95

THE TEN BOOKS OF ARCHITECTURE: The 1755 Leoni Edition, Leon Battista Alberti. Rare classic helped introduce the glories of ancient architecture to the Renaissance. 68 black-and-white plates. 336pp. 8⅜ × 11¼. 25239-6 Pa. $14.95

MISS MACKENZIE, Anthony Trollope. Minor masterpieces by Victorian master unmasks many truths about life in 19th-century England. First inexpensive edition in years. 392pp. 5⅜ × 8½. 25201-9 Pa. $7.95

THE RIME OF THE ANCIENT MARINER, Gustave Doré, Samuel Taylor Coleridge. Dramatic engravings considered by many to be his greatest work. The terrifying space of the open sea, the storms and whirlpools of an unknown ocean, the ice of Antarctica, more—all rendered in a powerful, chilling manner. Full text. 38 plates. 77pp. 9¼ × 12. 22305-1 Pa. $4.95

THE EXPEDITIONS OF ZEBULON MONTGOMERY PIKE, Zebulon Montgomery Pike. Fascinating first-hand accounts (1805-6) of exploration of Mississippi River, Indian wars, capture by Spanish dragoons, much more. 1,088pp. 5⅜ × 8½. 25254-X, 25255-8 Pa. Two-vol. set $23.90

A CONCISE HISTORY OF PHOTOGRAPHY: Third Revised Edition, Helmut Gernsheim. Best one-volume history—camera obscura, photochemistry, daguerreotypes, evolution of cameras, film, more. Also artistic aspects—landscape, portraits, fine art, etc. 281 black-and-white photographs. 26 in color. 176pp. 8⅜ × 11¼. 25128-4 Pa. $12.95

THE DORÉ BIBLE ILLUSTRATIONS, Gustave Doré. 241 detailed plates from the Bible: the Creation scenes, Adam and Eve, Flood, Babylon, battle sequences, life of Jesus, etc. Each plate is accompanied by the verses from the King James version of the Bible. 241pp. 9 × 12. 23004-X Pa. $8.95

HUGGER-MUGGER IN THE LOUVRE, Elliot Paul. Second Homer Evans mystery-comedy. Theft at the Louvre involves sleuth in hilarious, madcap caper. "A knockout."—Books. 336pp. 5⅜ × 8½. 25185-3 Pa. $5.95

FLATLAND, E. A. Abbott. Intriguing and enormously popular science-fiction classic explores the complexities of trying to survive as a two-dimensional being in a three-dimensional world. Amusingly illustrated by the author. 16 illustrations. 103pp. 5⅜ × 8½. 20001-9 Pa. $2.00

THE HISTORY OF THE LEWIS AND CLARK EXPEDITION, Meriwether Lewis and William Clark, edited by Elliott Coues. Classic edition of Lewis and Clark's day-by-day journals that later became the basis for U.S. claims to Oregon and the West. Accurate and invaluable geographical, botanical, biological, meteorological and anthropological material. Total of 1,508pp. 5⅜ × 8½. 21268-8, 21269-6, 21270-X Pa. Three-vol. set $25.50

LANGUAGE, TRUTH AND LOGIC, Alfred J. Ayer. Famous, clear introduction to Vienna, Cambridge schools of Logical Positivism. Role of philosophy, elimination of metaphysics, nature of analysis, etc. 160pp. 5⅜ × 8½. (Available in U.S. and Canada only) 20010-8 Pa. $2.95

MATHEMATICS FOR THE NONMATHEMATICIAN, Morris Kline. Detailed, college-level treatment of mathematics in cultural and historical context, with numerous exercises. For liberal arts students. Preface. Recommended Reading Lists. Tables. Index. Numerous black-and-white figures. xvi + 641pp. 5⅜ × 8½. 24823-2 Pa. $11.95

28 SCIENCE FICTION STORIES, H. G. Wells. Novels, *Star Begotten* and *Men Like Gods,* plus 26 short stories: "Empire of the Ants," "A Story of the Stone Age," "The Stolen Bacillus," "In the Abyss," etc. 915pp. 5⅜ × 8½. (Available in U.S. only) 20265-8 Cloth. $10.95

HANDBOOK OF PICTORIAL SYMBOLS, Rudolph Modley. 3,250 signs and symbols, many systems in full; official or heavy commercial use. Arranged by subject. Most in Pictorial Archive series. 143pp. 8⅛ × 11. 23357-X Pa. $5.95

INCIDENTS OF TRAVEL IN YUCATAN, John L. Stephens. Classic (1843) exploration of jungles of Yucatan, looking for evidences of Maya civilization. Travel adventures, Mexican and Indian culture, etc. Total of 669pp. 5⅜ × 8½. 20926-1, 20927-X Pa., Two-vol. set $9.90

DEGAS: An Intimate Portrait, Ambroise Vollard. Charming, anecdotal memoir by famous art dealer of one of the greatest 19th-century French painters. 14 black-and-white illustrations. Introduction by Harold L. Van Doren. 96pp. 5⅜ × 8½.
25131-4 Pa. $3.95

PERSONAL NARRATIVE OF A PILGRIMAGE TO ALMANDINAH AND MECCAH, Richard Burton. Great travel classic by remarkably colorful personality. Burton, disguised as a Moroccan, visited sacred shrines of Islam, narrowly escaping death. 47 illustrations. 959pp. 5⅜ × 8½.　21217-3, 21218-1 Pa., Two-vol. set $17.90

PHRASE AND WORD ORIGINS, A. H. Holt. Entertaining, reliable, modern study of more than 1,200 colorful words, phrases, origins and histories. Much unexpected information. 254pp. 5⅜ × 8½.　20758-7 Pa. $4.95

THE RED THUMB MARK, R. Austin Freeman. In this first Dr. Thorndyke case, the great scientific detective draws fascinating conclusions from the nature of a single fingerprint. Exciting story, authentic science. 320pp. 5⅜ × 8½. (Available in U.S. only)　25210-8 Pa. $5.95

AN EGYPTIAN HIEROGLYPHIC DICTIONARY, E. A. Wallis Budge. Monumental work containing about 25,000 words or terms that occur in texts ranging from 3000 B.C. to 600 A.D. Each entry consists of a transliteration of the word, the word in hieroglyphs, and the meaning in English. 1,314pp. 6⅜ × 10.
23615-3, 23616-1 Pa., Two-vol. set $27.90

THE COMPLEAT STRATEGYST: Being a Primer on the Theory of Games of Strategy, J. D. Williams. Highly entertaining classic describes, with many illustrated examples, how to select best strategies in conflict situations. Prefaces. Appendices. xvi + 268pp. 5⅜ × 8½.　25101-2 Pa. $5.95

THE ROAD TO OZ, L. Frank Baum. Dorothy meets the Shaggy Man, little Button-Bright and the Rainbow's beautiful daughter in this delightful trip to the magical Land of Oz. 272pp. 5⅜ × 8.　25208-6 Pa. $4.95

POINT AND LINE TO PLANE, Wassily Kandinsky. Seminal exposition of role of point, line, other elements in non-objective painting. Essential to understanding 20th-century art. 127 illustrations. 192pp. 6½ × 9¼.　23808-3 Pa. $4.50

LADY ANNA, Anthony Trollope. Moving chronicle of Countess Lovel's bitter struggle to win for herself and daughter Anna their rightful rank and fortune—perhaps at cost of sanity itself. 384pp. 5⅜ × 8½.　24669-8 Pa. $6.95

EGYPTIAN MAGIC, E. A. Wallis Budge. Sums up all that is known about magic in Ancient Egypt: the role of magic in controlling the gods, powerful amulets that warded off evil spirits, scarabs of immortality, use of wax images, formulas and spells, the secret name, much more. 253pp. 5⅜ × 8½.　22681-6 Pa. $4.00

THE DANCE OF SIVA, Ananda Coomaraswamy. Preeminent authority unfolds the vast metaphysic of India: the revelation of her art, conception of the universe, social organization, etc. 27 reproductions of art masterpieces. 192pp. 5⅜ × 8½.
24817-8 Pa. $5.95

CHRISTMAS CUSTOMS AND TRADITIONS, Clement A. Miles. Origin, evolution, significance of religious, secular practices. Caroling, gifts, yule logs, much more. Full, scholarly yet fascinating; non-sectarian. 400pp. 5⅜ × 8½.
23354-5 Pa. $6.50

THE HUMAN FIGURE IN MOTION, Eadweard Muybridge. More than 4,500 stopped-action photos, in action series, showing undraped men, women, children jumping, lying down, throwing, sitting, wrestling, carrying, etc. 390pp. 7⅞ × 10⅝.
20204-6 Cloth. $19.95

THE MAN WHO WAS THURSDAY, Gilbert Keith Chesterton. Witty, fast-paced novel about a club of anarchists in turn-of-the-century London. Brilliant social, religious, philosophical speculations. 128pp. 5⅜ × 8½.
25121-7 Pa. $3.95

A CEZANNE SKETCHBOOK: Figures, Portraits, Landscapes and Still Lifes, Paul Cezanne. Great artist experiments with tonal effects, light, mass, other qualities in over 100 drawings. A revealing view of developing master painter, precursor of Cubism. 102 black-and-white illustrations. 144pp. 8¾ × 6⅝.
24790-2 Pa. $5.95

AN ENCYCLOPEDIA OF BATTLES: Accounts of Over 1,560 Battles from 1479 B.C. to the Present, David Eggenberger. Presents essential details of every major battle in recorded history, from the first battle of Megiddo in 1479 B.C. to Grenada in 1984. List of Battle Maps. New Appendix covering the years 1967–1984. Index. 99 illustrations. 544pp. 6½ × 9¼.
24913-1 Pa. $14.95

AN ETYMOLOGICAL DICTIONARY OF MODERN ENGLISH, Ernest Weekley. Richest, fullest work, by foremost British lexicographer. Detailed word histories. Inexhaustible. Total of 856pp. 6½ × 9¼.
21873-2, 21874-0 Pa., Two-vol. set $17.00

WEBSTER'S AMERICAN MILITARY BIOGRAPHIES, edited by Robert McHenry. Over 1,000 figures who shaped 3 centuries of American military history. Detailed biographies of Nathan Hale, Douglas MacArthur, Mary Hallaren, others. Chronologies of engagements, more. Introduction. Addenda. 1,033 entries in alphabetical order. xi + 548pp. 6½ × 9¼. (Available in U.S. only)
24758-9 Pa. $11.95

LIFE IN ANCIENT EGYPT, Adolf Erman. Detailed older account, with much not in more recent books: domestic life, religion, magic, medicine, commerce, and whatever else needed for complete picture. Many illustrations. 597pp. 5⅜ × 8½.
22632-8 Pa. $8.50

HISTORIC COSTUME IN PICTURES, Braun & Schneider. Over 1,450 costumed figures shown, covering a wide variety of peoples: kings, emperors, nobles, priests, servants, soldiers, scholars, townsfolk, peasants, merchants, courtiers, cavaliers, and more. 256pp. 8⅜ × 11¼.
23150-X Pa. $7.95

THE NOTEBOOKS OF LEONARDO DA VINCI, edited by J. P. Richter. Extracts from manuscripts reveal great genius; on painting, sculpture, anatomy, sciences, geography, etc. Both Italian and English. 186 ms. pages reproduced, plus 500 additional drawings, including studies for *Last Supper, Sforza* monument, etc. 860pp. 7⅞ × 10¾. (Available in U.S. only) 22572-0, 22573-9 Pa., Two-vol. set $25.90

THE ART NOUVEAU STYLE BOOK OF ALPHONSE MUCHA: All 72 Plates from "Documents Decoratifs" in Original Color, Alphonse Mucha. Rare copyright-free design portfolio by high priest of Art Nouveau. Jewelry, wallpaper, stained glass, furniture, figure studies, plant and animal motifs, etc. Only complete one-volume edition. 80pp. 9⅜ × 12¼.   24044-4 Pa. $8.95

ANIMALS: 1,419 COPYRIGHT-FREE ILLUSTRATIONS OF MAMMALS, BIRDS, FISH, INSECTS, ETC., edited by Jim Harter. Clear wood engravings present, in extremely lifelike poses, over 1,000 species of animals. One of the most extensive pictorial sourcebooks of its kind. Captions. Index. 284pp. 9 × 12.
23766-4 Pa. $9.95

OBELISTS FLY HIGH, C. Daly King. Masterpiece of American detective fiction, long out of print, involves murder on a 1935 transcontinental flight—"a very thrilling story"—NY Times. Unabridged and unaltered republication of the edition published by William Collins Sons & Co. Ltd., London, 1935. 288pp. 5⅜ × 8½. (Available in U.S. only)   25036-9 Pa. $4.95

VICTORIAN AND EDWARDIAN FASHION: A Photographic Survey, Alison Gernsheim. First fashion history completely illustrated by contemporary photographs. Full text plus 235 photos, 1840–1914, in which many celebrities appear. 240pp. 6½ × 9¼.   24205-6 Pa. $6.00

THE ART OF THE FRENCH ILLUSTRATED BOOK, 1700–1914, Gordon N. Ray. Over 630 superb book illustrations by Fragonard, Delacroix, Daumier, Doré, Grandville, Manet, Mucha, Steinlen, Toulouse-Lautrec and many others. Preface. Introduction. 633 halftones. Indices of artists, authors & titles, binders and provenances. Appendices. Bibliography. 608pp. 8⅜ × 11¼.   25086-5 Pa. $24.95

THE WONDERFUL WIZARD OF OZ, L. Frank Baum. Facsimile in full color of America's finest children's classic. 143 illustrations by W. W. Denslow. 267pp. 5⅜ × 8½.   20691-2 Pa. $5.95

FRONTIERS OF MODERN PHYSICS: New Perspectives on Cosmology, Relativity, Black Holes and Extraterrestrial Intelligence, Tony Rothman, et al. For the intelligent layman. Subjects include: cosmological models of the universe; black holes; the neutrino; the search for extraterrestrial intelligence. Introduction. 46 black-and-white illustrations. 192pp. 5⅜ × 8½.   24587-X Pa. $6.95

THE FRIENDLY STARS, Martha Evans Martin & Donald Howard Menzel. Classic text marshalls the stars together in an engaging, non-technical survey, presenting them as sources of beauty in night sky. 23 illustrations. Foreword. 2 star charts. Index. 147pp. 5⅜ × 8½.   21099-5 Pa. $3.50

FADS AND FALLACIES IN THE NAME OF SCIENCE, Martin Gardner. Fair, witty appraisal of cranks, quacks, and quackeries of science and pseudoscience: hollow earth, Velikovsky, orgone energy, Dianetics, flying saucers, Bridey Murphy, food and medical fads, etc. Revised, expanded In the Name of Science. "A very able and even-tempered presentation."—The New Yorker. 363pp. 5⅜ × 8.
20394-8 Pa. $5.95

ANCIENT EGYPT: ITS CULTURE AND HISTORY, J. E Manchip White. From pre-dynastics through Ptolemies: society, history, political structure, religion, daily life, literature, cultural heritage. 48 plates. 217pp. 5⅜ × 8½.   22548-8 Pa. $4.95

CATALOG OF DOVER BOOKS

SIR HARRY HOTSPUR OF HUMBLETHWAITE, Anthony Trollope. Incisive, unconventional psychological study of a conflict between a wealthy baronet, his idealistic daughter, and their scapegrace cousin. The 1870 novel in its first inexpensive edition in years. 250pp. 5⅜ × 8½. 24953-0 Pa. $4.95

LASERS AND HOLOGRAPHY, Winston E. Kock. Sound introduction to burgeoning field, expanded (1981) for second edition. Wave patterns, coherence, lasers, diffraction, zone plates, properties of holograms, recent advances. 84 illustrations. 160pp. 5⅜ × 8¼. (Except in United Kingdom) 24041-X Pa. $3.50

INTRODUCTION TO ARTIFICIAL INTELLIGENCE: SECOND, EN-LARGED EDITION, Philip C. Jackson, Jr. Comprehensive survey of artificial intelligence—the study of how machines (computers) can be made to act intelligently. Includes introductory and advanced material. Extensive notes updating the main text. 132 black-and-white illustrations. 512pp. 5⅜ × 8½. 24864-X Pa. $8.95

HISTORY OF INDIAN AND INDONESIAN ART, Ananda K. Coomaraswamy. Over 400 illustrations illuminate classic study of Indian art from earliest Harappa finds to early 20th century. Provides philosophical, religious and social insights. 304pp. 6⅜ × 9⅜. 25005-9 Pa. $8.95

THE GOLEM, Gustav Meyrink. Most famous supernatural novel in modern European literature, set in Ghetto of Old Prague around 1890. Compelling story of mystical experiences, strange transformations, profound terror. 13 black-and-white illustrations. 224pp. 5⅜ × 8½. (Available in U.S. only) 25025-3 Pa. $5.95

ARMADALE, Wilkie Collins. Third great mystery novel by the author of *The Woman in White* and *The Moonstone*. Original magazine version with 40 illustrations. 597pp. 5⅜ × 8½. 23429-0 Pa. $7.95

PICTORIAL ENCYCLOPEDIA OF HISTORIC ARCHITECTURAL PLANS, DETAILS AND ELEMENTS: With 1,880 Line Drawings of Arches, Domes, Doorways, Facades, Gables, Windows, etc., John Theodore Haneman. Sourcebook of inspiration for architects, designers, others. Bibliography. Captions. 141pp. 9 × 12. 24605-1 Pa. $6.95

BENCHLEY LOST AND FOUND, Robert Benchley. Finest humor from early 30's, about pet peeves, child psychologists, post office and others. Mostly unavailable elsewhere. 73 illustrations by Peter Arno and others. 183pp. 5⅜ × 8½. 22410-4 Pa. $3.95

ERTÉ GRAPHICS, Erté. Collection of striking color graphics: *Seasons, Alphabet, Numerals, Aces* and *Precious Stones*. 50 plates, including 4 on covers. 48pp. 9⅜ × 12¼. 23580-7 Pa. $6.95

THE JOURNAL OF HENRY D. THOREAU, edited by Bradford Torrey, F. H. Allen. Complete reprinting of 14 volumes, 1837-61, over two million words; the sourcebooks for *Walden*, etc. Definitive. All original sketches, plus 75 photographs. 1,804pp. 8½ × 12¼. 20312-3, 20313-1 Cloth., Two-vol. set $80.00

CASTLES: THEIR CONSTRUCTION AND HISTORY, Sidney Toy. Traces castle development from ancient roots. Nearly 200 photographs and drawings illustrate moats, keeps, baileys, many other features. Caernarvon, Dover Castles, Hadrian's Wall, Tower of London, dozens more. 256pp. 5⅜ × 8¼. 24898-4 Pa. $5.95

AMERICAN CLIPPER SHIPS: 1833–1858, Octavius T. Howe & Frederick C. Matthews. Fully-illustrated, encyclopedic review of 352 clipper ships from the period of America's greatest maritime supremacy. Introduction. 109 halftones. 5 black-and-white line illustrations. Index. Total of 928pp. 5⅜ × 8½.
25115-2, 25116-0 Pa., Two-vol. set $17.90

TOWARDS A NEW ARCHITECTURE, Le Corbusier. Pioneering manifesto by great architect, near legendary founder of "International School." Technical and aesthetic theories, views on industry, economics, relation of form to function, "mass-production spirit," much more. Profusely illustrated. Unabridged translation of 13th French edition. Introduction by Frederick Etchells. 320pp. 6⅛ × 9¼. (Available in U.S. only) 25023-7 Pa. $8.95

THE BOOK OF KELLS, edited by Blanche Cirker. Inexpensive collection of 32 full-color, full-page plates from the greatest illuminated manuscript of the Middle Ages, painstakingly reproduced from rare facsimile edition. Publisher's Note. Captions. 32pp. 9⅜ × 12¼. 24345-1 Pa. $4.50

BEST SCIENCE FICTION STORIES OF H. G. WELLS, H. G. Wells. Full novel *The Invisible Man*, plus 17 short stories: "The Crystal Egg," "Aepyornis Island," "The Strange Orchid," etc. 303pp. 5⅜ × 8½. (Available in U.S. only)
21531-8 Pa. $4.95

AMERICAN SAILING SHIPS: Their Plans and History, Charles G. Davis. Photos, construction details of schooners, frigates, clippers, other sailcraft of 18th to early 20th centuries—plus entertaining discourse on design, rigging, nautical lore, much more. 137 black-and-white illustrations. 240pp. 6⅛ × 9¼.
24658-2 Pa. $5.95

ENTERTAINING MATHEMATICAL PUZZLES, Martin Gardner. Selection of author's favorite conundrums involving arithmetic, money, speed, etc., with lively commentary. Complete solutions. 112pp. 5⅜ × 8½. 25211-6 Pa. $2.95
THE WILL TO BELIEVE, HUMAN IMMORTALITY, William James. Two books bound together. Effect of irrational on logical, and arguments for human immortality. 402pp. 5⅜ × 8½. 20291-7 Pa. $7.50

THE HAUNTED MONASTERY and THE CHINESE MAZE MURDERS, Robert Van Gulik. 2 full novels by Van Gulik continue adventures of Judge Dee and his companions. An evil Taoist monastery, seemingly supernatural events; overgrown topiary maze that hides strange crimes. Set in 7th-century China. 27 illustrations. 328pp. 5⅜ × 8½. 23502-5 Pa. $5.00

CELEBRATED CASES OF JUDGE DEE (DEE GOONG AN), translated by Robert Van Gulik. Authentic 18th-century Chinese detective novel; Dee and associates solve three interlocked cases. Led to Van Gulik's own stories with same characters. Extensive introduction. 9 illustrations. 237pp. 5⅜ × 8½.
23337-5 Pa. $4.95

Prices subject to change without notice.
Available at your book dealer or write for free catalog to Dept. GI, Dover Publications, Inc., 31 East 2nd St., Mineola, N.Y. 11501. Dover publishes more than 175 books each year on science, elementary and advanced mathematics, biology, music, art, literary history, social sciences and other areas.

Balm

Basil

Chervil

Borage

Cinnamon

Coriander

Garlic

Mint

Rosemary

Nutmeg

Vanilla

Wintergreen